60

'We've woven swans into our folk-lore, legends, music and art, but these birds are suffering and dying daily. They get hit by boats, stoned by vandals and killed by anglers who discard tackle on the river banks . . . *White Spirit, Fly Free* . . . tells of the work of Len and Sheila Baker, who run a Swan Rescue Service. It's a bittersweet tale: you'll shed a tear or two, but there's also laughter and happiness'
Woman's World

'A deeply affecting book'
Sheffield Morning Telegraph

D1796256

'An inspiring book, one that can cause tears and hope in the mind of the reader. It is certainly a book that I will read again – and savour'
Cork Examiner

Pamela Townsend, a Londoner, has been a journalist all her working life. Starting as a newspaper reporter, she quickly discovered that she found people far more interesting than news, and redirected her career to towards feature writing. She is now an established freelance writer, working for various publications, but specializing in women's magazines. *White Spirit, Fly Free* is her second book.

Her innate interest in people and their cultures, and latterly in animals and their conservation, has caused her to travel widely across the world, including the Far East, India and Pakistan. Her travelling companion is usually her husband, also a journalist.

Pamela lives in Richmond-upon-Thames, Surrey.

White Spirit, Fly Free

One man's fight to save Britain's swans

Pamela Townsend

CORGI BOOKS

WHITE SPIRIT, FLY FREE

A CORGI BOOK 0 552 12657 8

Originally published in Great Britain by
Sidgwick & Jackson Limited

PRINTING HISTORY

Sidgwick & Jackson edition published 1984
Corgi edition published 1985

Copyright © 1984 Pamela Townsend

All the poetry in this book, unless otherwise stated,
is by Len Baker.
The line drawings are by Eddie Bush.

This book is set in 10/11pt Plantin

Corgi Books are published by
Transworld Publishers Ltd.,
Century House, 61-63 Uxbridge Road,
Ealing, London W5 5SA

Printed and bound in Great Britain by
Cox & Wyman Ltd., Reading, Berks.

Contents

Author's Acknowledgments

While most of the facts in this book originated from Len Baker, other people kindly responded when specific information was needed. My particular thanks go to Alan Hunt, the clinical biochemist at the MAFF veterinary investigation centre at Sutton Bonnington; not only had he diligently logged his swan post-mortems over the years but he was prepared to share his findings with me, patiently leading me into his area of specialized knowledge. I am grateful for the assistance given by David Glue at the British Trust for Ornithology, and to Joe Hardman, the keen amateur lover of swans who has done so much at Stratford. Sylvia Bruce Wilmore's research into the mythology and history of swans for her own book *Swans of the World* was of invaluable help to me and pointed me in many right directions.

Finally to A.E., the most important of all, thank you for your loving support and patience.

Foreword

In writing this book I entered a world previously unknown to me. I have learned more about swans in the past months than I ever dreamed of knowing in the whole of my life. Seeing at first hand the tragic state they are in I have been touched by the shameful things that we, humankind, are doing in general to the wildlife of our country, our planet. To write conservation articles, as I have done for years, is one thing. To see someone like Len Baker, and there are other people like him in other fields, actually roll up his sleeves and, with very little help from anyone else, try to stop the suffering, is quite another. It is considered wise to say that the pen is mightier than the sword, but when it comes to saving our animals and our wildlife I disagree. Words will certainly alert, but we can write and talk till there are no free-roaming cows left to come home.

We need those crusading warriors, we need them quickly. We need people in their thousands armed with caring hearts and a correct sense of priorities. We need to heal the wounds that have been mainly caused by human greed and exploitation, and to learn that humans do not come first. We must learn to share or there will be nothing left to share. We could say that our ancestors damaged this planet and its wildlife in ignorance, for they did not have the data and expertise that are now at our fingertips. We have no excuses.

In the words of a folk song, 'God gave life to the animals . . . it's their world too.' I pray that this book, about just one hardhit species on this earth, will contribute something in the fight for reason and universal love.

Pamela Townsend
London, 1983

Setting the Scene

I was off guard.
You took, without asking,
A selection of my emotions.
You toyed with them
For a while.
Then you scattered them
Like tiny fragments
Of burnt paper
In the wind.
I feel no bitterness
Toward you for your action.
I was,
And am,
Captivated
By your spiritual
Trickery.
I love you, swan.

Dawn seems to arrive very quickly in East Anglia, that flat, open chunk of land on the east coast of Britain, lying vulnerable and outstretched beneath a vast sky. For some inexplicable reason one is more aware of the elements there: more aware of the sky's changing moods, of the closeness of nature; aware of the wind that seems to be constantly blowing, be it gentle breeze or severe North Sea blast.

To look up and see a swan in full flight is a breathtaking experience anywhere in the world. In East Anglia, though far from being an everyday occurrence, it is not a surprising sight, for this flat, seductive corner of England has been the home of swans

11

for many centuries. They have played on the wind there for many, many years, have nested, had their families, taught their cygnets the joys of flight, all in their own harmless, beautiful way. Swans have brought magic to this planet; they have haunted composers, inspired writers and left their mark on the mythology of countries from Wales to Australia.

One bright, red-skyed Norfolk dawn in April 1978 a very special swan was playing the Norfolk winds. Later to become known as Marlon, he will figure largely in this book.

On that April morning he was a proud father for the first and only time, and he was showing off. His wing-span was an impressive 8 feet 3½ inches; up and down, round and round, he circled over his territory on the River Bure that runs through the Norfolk Broads before entering the North Sea at Great Yarmouth. Swooping with triumphant calls, he seemed to want the world to know how clever he had been. Seven beautiful cygnets were safely tucked up with their mother in the nest on the river, and Marlon was tellling the world all about it.

But meanwhile, not far away, some swans were in trouble. The swans in Ipswich Docks had little to make them swoop with joy, in fact many were too weak to fly at all. Victims of man's commercialism, they had made the tragic mistake of settling on what to them must have looked a very attractive estuary. But they did not know about pollution, or about the lack of reeds which they need in order to survive; they did not know that oil from the ships would ruin their plumage and possibly kill them if they tried to preen, or that the discharge from dockside factories had poisoned their water.

In short they were starving and they were sick. At that time there were about sixty swans in Ipswich Docks, begging and scraping a life that should never have befallen such a wonderful bird. That number is gradually decreasing and it is possible that by the time you read this book there will be no swans there at all. Those that have not died will have been found new homes, for their plight became the urgent priority of a husband-and-wife team who have given their life, their energy and their money to help stop the suffering of Britain's swans.

Len and Sheila Baker created and now run the Swan Rescue Service. The fact that they had to do so is a blot on the copybook of humankind and sad proof of what we are doing to the wildlife of this planet. For alongside elephants, whales, seals, rhinos and countless other species, swans are suffering at the hands of man. Unable to cope with the hazards of the twentieth century, they are undergoing pain and distress that is almost beyond belief, and in some areas their numbers have decreased alarmingly.

In many places, and East Anglia is one of these, this noble bird, the largest in England, has been turned into a mucky, bedraggled hobo. Often forced to beg for food, some of the swans, like those at Ipswich Docks, do not even know what fresh water tastes like. When they are not struggling against pollution, lead-poisoning and starvation they are being rammed by boats or having stones hurled at them.

This book is about swans. It is not a textbook or a veterinary guide. It is not about the birds' nesting habits or wing-spans or digestive systems; many books have already been written on these subjects. It is about the swans of Britain as Len Baker knows them, for he lives with them. It is about their personalities, their suffering and the love and trust they have shown to him in abundance since he first got to know them six years ago.

The story tells of a unique relationship between man and bird, and of how together they are trying to work out problems, bond friendships and simply cope with the tragic circumstances in which they find themselves. Len, with Sheila beside him, works round the clock to save the lives of swans. In return the swans have brought them both magic moments and a richness that most of us would find difficult to understand.

I first met the Bakers when I was sent to write a feature about them for a national magazine. Being a somewhat cynical town-dweller, I thought they must be crazy. And perhaps they are. Perhaps you have to be slightly crazy to live and eat and sleep with swans; to give them all your money and let them dominate your life. But swan magic is contagious, and having got to know the Bakers and their work I could not help but catch a little of their madness. You can not help either your heart hurting when it sees what man is doing to the swans – innocent sufferers in a cruel, harsh environment.

All the swan knowledge in this book, unless otherwise stated, comes from Len Baker. I am merely a friend of the swans who has

13

written the book that Len would never have had time to write himself. The bulk of the money that we both earn from this book will be going directly to the swans, in the hope that it may buy their survival and ease their suffering. If things in this country continue as they are Len thinks the swans on our rivers will die out completely within a dozen years. But he has plans for them, and he has a dream, which you will read about later in the book.

Meanwhile I would like to introduce you to the world of swans. It is a world full of tears and sad moments, but of joy and pleasure too. And hope also. For we cannot sit back and let our beautiful swans suffer as they do now. If this book helps to alert you, the general public, to the swans' tragic plight then it will have done some good. It will as well, I hope, bring you a little swan magic.

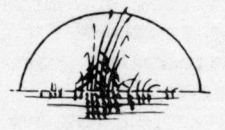

Swan Magic

I will play the swan,
And die in music.

William Shakespeare
Othello, *Act V scene 2*

Contrary to myth, the mute swan does not sing, not even before it dies. And yet it has pleased man down the centuries to believe that in some mysterious moment, perhaps when no human is around, the swan bursts forth in song to herald its own death. Like Shakespeare, Byron too was charmed by this idea, and in 'The Isles of Greece' wrote:

Place me on Sunium's marbled steep
Where nothing, save waves and I,
May hear our mutual murmurs sweep;
There, swan-like, let me sing and die.

For some reason man has given the swan a very special place in his mythology and his thoughts. Why? The swan is a beautiful bird, it is true, with its dazzling white plumage, but the peacock or flamingo, to name just two, rival it in appearance. It is an impressive size, but so too are other birds. It has grace and charm, and an admirable character, so too do other birds. Perhaps it is the way the swan dips its slender neck in silent humility; or the way it bows its head as if in prayer. Perhaps it is the all-knowing eyes which seem to carry within them knowledge of bygone days and cultures. Perhaps it is the nonchalant flick of the head, that with superior motion and just the right touch of

15

arrogance, turns the swan around and sends him gliding away from you, bored with the attention given to him by a human.

No one knows the answer to the swan's secret, But they have cleverly worked their way into our legends in a way that no other bird has done. Art as far back as the Stone Age has depicted swans. Rock carvings of swans have been found in Russia, and paintings on cave walls, dated around 18,000 BC have been found in Spain, France and Italy.

Perhaps the swan's pure white plumage and its link with purity has something to do with the magic. Yet in Australia the aborigines were enchanted by their own native black swan, which was thought to be the bird of the Great One. White swans do appear in Australian folklore, however. In one tale a magician named Wurrunnah wanted to divert the attention of a tribe of women while his men raided their camp. So he turned his two brothers into white swans, which duly enchanted the women. The raid was successful and the celebrating Wurrunnah forgot about his brothers, who were attacked by eagles which ripped off their feathers and injured them. But a flock of crows, seeing the sorry state of the two plucked swans, pulled feathers from their own breasts and let them fall down on to the naked swans. Legend has it that this is why Australian swans are black, their crimson beaks resulting from the blood of their wounds.

As far back as human history can trace, swans have been linked with death and the soul. The different peoples of Russia, particularly those from Siberia, have contributed much to the mystical reputation of the swan. Some have effigies of swans erected on poles around their coffins, others have the swan as their totem. Some Siberian tribes think that it is dangerous even to point at a swan and that to handle a feather is sinful, while others believe that death will come to the slayer of a swan. The Buriats of central Siberia see the swan as the mother of their race, and hold an annual festival at which they drink and pray to the bird.

The swan-maiden myth is believed to have originated in Siberia, and the Buriats do have embedded in their culture a tale based on the standard swan-maiden theme. Their story is that one day three swans arrived at a lake, discarded their feathers on the bank and went for a swim. A passing hunter took one of the feather cloaks and when its owner, now a beautiful maiden, emerged from the water, he married her. Many years later he allowed his wife to try on her swan feathers and she flew away through the smoke-hole of their tent.

This idea of the metamorphosis from swan to beautiful maiden appears in many mythologies of different peoples around the world. Though it varies from country to country the theme remains generally the same, the half-mortal, half-supernatural maiden having to repossess her feather robe, and often her crown, chain or ring too, before returning to her swan form. The story appears again and again throughout Europe and Asia, Africa and the Far East: the Celtic and Teutonic peoples embody it within their legends and so too, it is thought, do the Zulus. Even the smoke-hole in the tent appears in stories far from Siberia. In one Irish legend the heroine flies out of the smoke-hole of her mortal husband's castle. Carried away by her lover, the two of them, as swans, fly to a fairy land where she becomes queen.

Perhaps the most famous rendering of the swan-maiden story is in the ballet *Swan Lake*. Tchaikovsky, like so many others, was obviously bewitched by the story and his music has made the swan-maiden legend immortal. The famous Russian ballerina Pavlova, who gained great acclaim for her 'dying swan', studied swans at close quarters in order to capture their every movement. So intoxicated did she become with these beautiful birds that she kept a pair of mute swans on the lake of her London home.

Greek mythology abounds with swan connections, and in one we are told why the mute swan droops his head so mournfully. Cygnus, son of Poseidon the Greek god of the sea, had a close friend who angered the great god Zeus by riding his father's sun-chariot recklessly across the sky. Zeus hurled a thunderbolt at the chariot which, with Cygnus' friend still on board, was flung into the river. Cygnus dived in to save him, and so many times did he attempt to gather up the charred remains of his friend that when he eventually died from grief the gods took pity on him and allowed him to haunt the river as a swan. The constellation of stars, Cygnus the Swan, is said to have been named after him when he was later transformed into a star. To this day the ornithological name for the mute swan is *Cygnus olor*.

One of the most famous Greek legends is the story of Leda and

Zeus. Leda, having slept with her husband, was seduced on the same night by the great god Zeus, who was disguised as a swan. As a result of her double conception Leda gave birth to two pairs of swans, each pair enclosd in an egg. Two children were of Zeus, and two were the children of her husband.

The story of Leda has captured the imagination of many an artist. Yeats wrote a poem called 'Leda and the Swan':

> *A sudden blow, the great wings beating still*
> *Above the staggering girl, her thighs caressed*
> *By the dark webs, her nape caught in his bill,*
> *He holds her helpless, breast upon his breast.*

Michelangelo also used the subject in one of his paintings, which although known to have been at one time in the possession of the King of France is now untraceable. The National Gallery in London has what is assumed to be an old copy of the original Michelangelo.

When Apollo, the son of Zeus and Leto (Leda) and the twin of Artemis (Diana), was born swans encircled the birthplace seven times. Zeus showered gifts upon his children, including two chariots drawn by swans. It was in his swan-chariot that Apollo headed for Delphi, the place of his temple, but on the way he stopped for one year in the swans' country on the edge of the ocean. The people there made him their god, and according to Greek legend Apollo's soul passed into a swan. This is said to be why the Worshipful Company of Musicians has a swan on its coat of arms – as a tribute to the Greek god of music.

Aphrodite (Venus), the goddess of love, is said to have travelled to Greece in a chariot drawn by swans. The swan is sacred to Venus as the image of chaste nudity and immaculate whiteness. In erotic symbolism the swan's long phallic neck is said to represent the generative power of the male, while the silky, white, rounded body represents the female.

The swan is to be found in Scandinavian mythology too. The sacred spring of Urd which lies beneath Yggdrasil, the great ash tree that binds together earth, heaven and hell with its roots and branches, was the home of the two swans from where all swans are said to have originated.

Finnish mythology captured the imagination of Sibelius, who put various legends to music, one of which is The Swan of Tuonela. The swan was said to swim and sing on a river that divided Tuonela, the land of death, from the land of the living. A young Nordic hero wanting to marry the girl he loved was told by her ugly old mother that he could only have her daughter if he shot the sacred swan with just one arrow. The young hero found the swan and was about to shoot when a blind shepherd, whom he had previously scorned, hurled a water snake at him. The hero fell into the river of death which carried him to Tuonela.

The Indian god Brahma, the Hindu creator of the universe, was called One Goose, or One Swan, and swans towed his chariot which was said to be swifter than thought. Buddha, too, is linked with a swan. As a young man he found a swan that had been injured by an arrow. When the hunter tried to claim his trophy he was told by Buddha that life belongs to him who saves it. Buddha nursed the injured bird, which stayed with him and helped him in his search for a way of life.

India is also the source of a very ancient version of the swan-maiden legend. Urvasi, a beautiful angel, deserted her husband when he broke a sacred custom. He eventually found her living on a lake with nymphs in the form of swans, but she refused to return to him.

Over the centuries the legend of a Swan Knight was to become as important as that of the swan-maiden. Like so many legends there is no way of telling how or when it began. The thirteenth-century poem 'Parsifal' by Wolfram Van Eschenbach portrays the Swan Knight as Lohengrin, son of Parsifal, who went in search of King Arthur and his Knights of the Holy Grail. Others have suggested that the true Swan Knight was an ancestor of the first Saxon Earl of Warwick.

The story that is said to have introduced, and popularized the Swan Knight legend involves seven children who were all born with golden chains around their necks. Their mother, a nymph, died and their father, the king, went away on a campaign. They were left in the charge of their grandmother, who tried to rid herself of them and took away their chains. All the children except the daughter changed into swans. The grief-stricken girl went in search of her father, who on his return forced his mother to confess her crime. When the chains were returned the sons resumed their human forms – all except one whose chain had been lost, who remained a swan for ever. The Swan Knight refused to leave his swan brother and wherever he travelled the two went together.

Wagner was among the many artists to be inspired by the Swan Knight, and his opera *Lohengrin* has immortalized the legend.

The web of mythology surrounding the Swan Knight is often contradictory. One version suggest that a son of the Swan Knight was Godfrey of Bouillon, leader of the First Crusade who became known as Protector of the Holy Sepulchre. The Swan Knight cult is widespread, always linked with powerful and important people, and there have been many claims by European families of descendancy from the Swan Knight. Many of those claiming descendancy took to wearing swan badges, while others, including English families, added the image of a swan to their family crests and wore it on their helmets. King John of France in the fourteenth century had swans as supporters for his shield and banners, and in 1476 King Christian of Denmark had a silver swan with a gold chain upon his seal.

Special swan feasts were held in honour of the Swan Knight. At one such banquet given by the Duke of Burgundy in 1453 the top table bore an eye-catching spectacle: a model ship in full sail drawn by a silver swan harnessed with a golden collar and long chain; inside stood an armed knight wearing a coat bearing the arms of Cleves, and at the end of the ship was a castle with a falcon floating in the river beneath. This scene represented the story of the knight who sailed down the Rhine to the Castle of Cleves, where he married the princess and was there the progenitor of the dukes of Cleves. One descendant was Anne of Cleves, the fourth wife of Henry VIII, who with her marriage brought her family's swan connections to the British Royal Family.

But swans had already carved an important place for themselves in British history long before the arrival of Anne of Cleves. King Edward I is thought to have founded an Order of Swans, for it was customary during his reign for knights to make their vows 'before the swan'. One particular feast for the swan held by Edward on Whit Sunday, 1306, is reported to have been the most splendid feast since Arthur was crowned at Caerleon. It copied the style of Arthurian banquets, in which elaborately decorated swans were carried in to the sound of trumpets and the knights then made their vows.

The swan-upping on the River Thames, which takes place during the third week of every July, is one of England's traditions. The numbers involved are small, and the interested parties are now only three: the monarch and the Worshipful Companies of Dyers and Vintners. Dressed in traditional costumes the watermen and lightermen, together with the Queen's Swan Keeper, take to the water to inspect and count the birds, including the summer's new cygnets. The royal birds are no longer marked, but those belonging to the Dyers and Vintners still are. They are the last remaining two swan marks – the final relics of the ancient custom of swan-marking that was once commonplace in this country.

The tradition of swan-marking, and the monarch's interest in it, reflect the unique place afforded to the swan in Britain. The origin of the royal connection is not clear. We know that the sturgeon, for example, was created a royal fish by Act of Parliament during the reign of Edward II, but there is no record of exactly how and when the swan was elevated to its lofty rank.

The writer N. F. Ticehurst, in his standard work *The Mute Swan in England* published in 1957, states that it was prior to 1186 that the swan in our country was given royal status. It was understood, Ticehurst tells us, that while a person could keep swans as captives on his own private waters, all others living on open and common water belong to the Crown. The Crown, however, could and did allow certain privileged people to keep swans on common waters, provided the birds were distinguished with the owner's own marking. After this, swan-marking – carried out by the scarring method of cutting into the skin of the beak – became widespread. It is recorded, for example, that in 1356 Edward III granted to the Warden and College of the King's Free Chapel of Windsor all unmarked swans using the river Thames between Oxford and London Bridge, for seven years. And in 1392 Richard II granted one of his knights all wild, unmarked swans in the county of Cambridge, for three years.

Commoners were also keeping swans. It is known that at the

21

time of the Norman Conquest swans were an important source of income to peasants living in wetland areas such as East Anglia. Unfortunately for them (and the swans) the bird, despite its royal and supernatural connections, was fast gaining in popularity as a tasty dish, and the rearing and selling of swans for food was becoming a lucrative business from which they were soon to be excluded.

Sylvia Bruce Wilmore, in her book *Swans of the World* first published in 1974, states that in 1274 the price of swan for food was fixed by the Statute Poltrice of the City of London at 3*s*. per bird. Compared to the price of goose which sold for 5*d*., best capon for 2½*d*. and a pheasant for 4*d*., the profit to be made in swan-keeping becomes obvious. By 1418 the price of swan varied from 3*s*. 6*d*. to 6*s*. 8*d*.

The increasing popularity of swan meat is shown by a record of a Christmas feast held at Winchester: in 1247 Henry III ordered 40 swans to be served; in 1251 he called for 125, which were collected from Northumberland to Lincoln.

The value of these birds could not be shared with the peasantry, and in the fifteenth century 'indiscriminate' ownership was stopped. In 1482 an Act of Swans stipulated that nobody could own a swan-mark and keep swans unless he owned freehold land and tenements to a certain high value. The Crown continued to use the granting of swan ownership to privileged peoples until the eighteenth century, when the custom of swan-marking died out.

The mark of the Dyers' Company (granted in 1473) and that of the Vintners' Company (granted in 1472) are the only two remaining, and the only royal swans now live on the Thames. The swans of Britain have returned to their wild state, cleverly retaining that rather special, privileged place in our hearts.

As in ancient days, to be associated with a swan will always be a compliment. To have swan-like grace and beauty is a flattery indeed. Every little ballerina will practise for hours to capture those special movements, those soft bends, that graceful pose. Not that the female has the monopoly on the swan. The Greek philosopher Pythagoras is thought to have been the first to claim that all good poets pass into swans at their death. Virgil was known as the 'Mantuan Swan', Homer as the 'Swan of Meander', while Ben Jonson was to call William Shakespeare the 'Sweet Swan of Avon'.

HM The Queen receives requests from all parts of the world for pairs of her breeding swans. The Lord Chamberlain's Office deals with these requests, and I am told that for the past three years, and for the foreseeable future, no such requests have been or will be granted. Due to the plight of swans in general in this country, and on the Thames in particular, Her Majesty has joined the band of conservationists working to save the swan.

Birth and Growth

There is a bend
In this very English river,
Where the willow
Kisses the water
And reeds dance
With their own reflections,
And whisper secrets
To each other
On the wings of the wind.
When all around you
Is darkness and pain
You can take refuge
In this place,
Even if it exists
Only in your
Own mind.

Len Baker was born in Chelsea, London, in 1935. He admits that he has always been 'a bit of an odd-bod'. Abandoned by his parents when he was ten years old, he was brought up in a London County Council orphanage. At fourteen he ran away and became a boarder in a Pimlico brothel at 12*s*.6*d*. a week, before being retrieved by the orphanage welfare staff.

The next year Len ran away again and slept rough on Platform 9 of Liverpool Street Station, before being unofficially adopted by a police constable who took pity on him. At seventeen, in desperate need of some stability and without a qualification to his name, he joined the Royal Air Force. He signed on for five years and learned the trade of jet engine fitter. He was based at RAF Coltishall in Norfolk, just a few miles from where he now runs his Swan Rescue Service.

It was at Coltishall that he met Sheila, who was a teleprint operator in WRAF communications. They were married in 1957. A year later they left the RAF and set themselves up in Norwich as owners of a motorcycle sales and repair shop. The business flourished, and within ten years they owned five shops, with Len doing some motorbike racing on the side.

Despite the fun of being his own boss, Len was restless. The restrictions and red tape involved in running a small business annoyed him, and besides, he had itchy feet. In 1968 the Bakers emigrated to Australia with their two daughters, hoping to begin a new life. And they were successful. Len, having started as a technical rep' for a plastics company, was very quickly made managing director. At this time the world was hit by an oil crisis which meant that polyester resin, which is made from petrol and was needed by Len's company, was in short supply. So Len was sent round the world with a brief to buy 65,000 tons of the resin. Leaving Sheila and the children in their lovely house next door to the Royal Melbourne Golf Club, he travelled thousands of miles, to Europe, the Soviet Union, Japan, India and North America. As he says:

> We had left England to get away from commercialism and the rat race, and I ended up being the business executive that I could never have been in England. I was earning the equivalent of £350 a week and had £70 a day expenses. I owned a beautiful air-conditioned car with tinted windows, we had a wonderful house, we had everything. It was like a dream.

In life, doors often open without us noticing them – or at least, with us not noticing them at the time – and a very important door in Len's life started to unlock in the transit lounge of Chicago airport. He got talking to a strange-looking man wearing a denim jacket, beads, Indian boots, a cowboy hat with silver eagles around the brim and a dog collar. He turned out to be a Roman Catholic priest from Taos in New Mexico, and he invited Len, should he ever be in the area, to visit *the* people. By that he meant the Indians.

A short time after that chance meeting Len did happen to be in the area, so he hired a car and drove to the mission where the priest lived.

And suddenly I found something I had been looking for all my life. I can only describe it as absolute peace, beautiful peace.

The priest was standing on the steps of the little mission church as I arrived. He was grinning like a kid as he welcomed me. He had his long black clothes on this time, with a single feather in his beautiful big hat. Five little raven-haired children ran up and grabbed hold of me and cuddled me; everyone was so happy that someone had come to visit them. I was completely overwhelmed by them. I felt I'd come to somewhere I was meant to be. They were a tribe of beautiful, gentle people and I spent four of the most important days of my life with them.

They were important in ways that at the time Len did not realize. One elderly Indian couple – the husband eighty-two and the wife seventy-nine – had a pair of scruffy, tame eagles which they allowed Len to befriend. Seeing his interest they took him into their little hut and showed him books on the care of eagles.

They showed me how to mend birds with birds, which was incredible. They showed me how to take a primary feather off a wing and cut it lengthways and make a splint for the same bird's leg. They would take oil from the preen gland of the bird, mix something with it, and use it as an eye ointment on the same bird. They would boil new feather roots to make a substance from the calcium in the quill and use that as a treatment for the bird. They said a bird would mend a bird, and that a bird would know how to mend himself. And they showed *me* how to mend birds.

Len was thrilled with these discoveries and had dreams of running the biggest eagle hospital in the world, but his plans did not gain favour with his Indian friends. His future was not with eagles, they told him. His destiny, they said, would lie with a big white bird.

Somewhat downhearted, Len left America to return to Melbourne. He didn't give those prophetic words much thought, nor did he really consider which big white bird the Indian couple could have meant.

I got into the car one hot Melbourne morning and the seat-belt burnt me because I'd left the car in the sun. And all of a sudden all I wanted in the world was to see a thrush on an English lawn. Of all the beautiful creatures that live in Australia, I just wanted to see a thrush and I couldn't buy it. I couldn't hear him singing, and I couldn't see dew on an English oak tree – it wasn't there.

Long discussions followed, and in 1975 the family arrived back in England. They had been in Australia for seven years. Like homing birds they headed for their beloved Norfolk; they were practically penniless, for although Len had been earning good money they had been living at a high standard.

There was little chance of walking straight into a managing directorship back in Britain, and besides, Len decided that he had experienced enough of the executive world. He wanted a more peaceful life, he wanted to live in the country not in a town, and he wanted a job with less responsibility. A vacancy for a fibreglass worker in a boatyard in Horning on the Broads suited him down to the ground, so he took it, and Sheila went to work in a small plastics factory. Eventually they settled in the rented cottage that was to become the centre of their life's work, although at this time they had no inkling of what that was to be.

Marlon was to become one of Len's closest swan friends. He was one of the first swans Len dealt with and was to teach Len much about swans and their ways. In fact, it had only been six months before meeting Marlon that Len had decided to move into swan rescue work. He used to spend his lunch breaks on the riverbank, just sitting and watching, fascinated by the hustle-bustle of nature at work all around him.

*   *   *

27

I used to watch a water vole. He used to come out of his little hole right opposite me and look up and down the river and sniff, and I used to throw bits of vegetation which he completely ignored. One day I had an apple and I threw him a piece of that and you've never seen a creature go so wild, he loved his apple. So every day I'd take him his apple and we would talk about all sorts of things, we'd put the world right together. Then one day we were chatting and I saw what I thought was a white plastic bag. It turned upside-down and two little black flippers came out of the water. It was a swan, and what I thought was an orange label was a beak. The swan was calling out, the most plaintive, distressing cry I'd ever heard.

I could see it was wrapped in something, but I couldn't reach it and I didn't really know what to do. I ran back to the boatyard, grabbed a boat-hook, tore back to the riverbank and pulled the swan in towards me. It was completely tied up in fishing line. It had a fishing hook in its back and its wings were tied down. Its feet had been badly cut by the line, they were in a terrible state.

I pulled it up on to the bank. I was quite frightened; I'd heard stories that a swan can break a man's arm, so I was a bit wary. I just sat holding it for what seemed ages. I tried to untangle the line, but I was clumsy and pulled out some of the feathers. I got 115 feet of line off that swan, which I've kept to this day. The hook wouldn't come out at first but I just kept pulling; a bit of skin came off and it bled for a while, but it stopped. When I'd finished I stood up and the swan sat motionless, it wouldn't move. I gave it a gentle push towards the water and it turned around and hissed angrily at me. It lifted its wings in aggression and then waddled off into the water and went down river without even looking round. I thought, 'That's gratitude.' It hurt me a little that it didn't even look round.

All this took about ten minutes, but it was to be the turning point in Len's life. A love affair had begun. He went back to the boatyard where he worked and told his friends that he had just untangled a swan. Oh yes, they said, swans are always getting caught up in fishing line. It appeared that no one actually looked after the swans. The people that Len asked thought the RSPCA cared for them; the RSPCA said they only went to incidents if the public called them. In other words, no one was actually responsible for the welfare of the hundreds of swans on the Broads. Len decided that he would be.

That was on 18 October 1977, the day that Swan Rescue was founded. At first Len and Sheila just kept an eye out for injured swans, then gradually the responsibility upon them grew heavier and they started to go out in the car and look for the birds. Straight after work in the evenings they would patrol the rivers and quaysides in the car, and gradually they became skilled at removing fishing line and hooks. Then they put a notice in their car window saying that they rescued swans, and slowly people started coming to them to tell of distressed swans in the vicinity. The momentum had begun and there was no going back now, even if they had wanted to.

It soon became apparent that their home, a detached cottage in Sparham, thirteen miles from Norwich, would have to become both hospital and convalescent home for the swans. The garden, which is nearly one-fifth of an acre, became the injured swans' haven, and as they got better, their playground too. Trying to mend injured swans on the riverside was better than nothing, but it was not ideal. The dull light of dusk or the beam from a car's headlight are not the best conditions under which to perform tricky operations, and swans that have suffered shock need nursing. The Bakers could often see that a swan was not in a fit state to be put straight back into the water. So they started taking swans home. Len slowly learned the art of swan-husbandry and Sheila, his chief assistant, became head nurse too; it was in her arms that the swans would lie all night, and often they died in her comforting lap.

The first inmate of the Bakers' swan home was Lady Wednesday, so named because she was rescued on that day. She had been found in a dyke by a policeman, who had telephoned Swan Rescue and given directions as to where she could be found. 'It was November and absolutely bitter. We took Lady Wednesday to a vet who told us she had a fractured pelvis, a broken leg and gangrene. The vet said kill her, but we weren't going to do that. After all, you wouldn't put down a human with those injuries.'

So they took Lady Wednesday home and nursed her for three

months. They gave her the antibiotics that the vet had prescribed, but for a long while she was unable to move. Every day Sheila would massage Lady Wednesday's legs and rub her body to keep the circulation going. She was a terrible mess: her left leg was broken in three places and part of a toe had to be cut away because it was so gangrenous. Nobody knew what fate had befallen her; Len assumed she had flown into a power cable.

Then one dark morning when Len was in the bathroom shaving, an excited Sheila came running in from the garden. 'She's moved, she's moved, Lady Wednesday's moved!'

The couple ran outside and yes, it was true, Lady Wednesday wasn't positioned as they had left her the night before. She must have moved of her own volition. They were ecstatic. Sheila took the day off work to be with her 'baby' and Len went to the boatyard as usual. 'At about 11 o'clock Sheila phoned me, and she was crying. Lady Wednesday had stood up and Sheila had seen her. It was fantastic. We were both overcome with emotion.'

Lady Wednesday was their first long-term successful patient and she was to become an integral part of the Swan Rescue team. She never flew back to freedom, for her injuries had been too great, but she lived out her days as surrogate mother to many injured cygnets. She was about seven years old and had probably been a mother many times herself, and she was a dab hand at rearing cygnets. She had her own pen in the Bakers' garden and during the eighteen months that she lived with them before her death she 'mothered' 118 cygnets. She taught them how to queue up for the food buckets, and shared with them all the little tricks that she had learned during her lifetime.

Quite soon the garden contained about twenty injured swans. Slowly they were taking over the Bakers' lives. They were both still working full-time, but getting up at 5 a.m. to tend the swans before work and going out in the car every evening to deal with new injured swans. The garden swans had to be fed daily, and bathed, for a swan will get arthritis if it is not regularly in water. At that time the Bakers did not even have a garden pool.

Sheila was earning £59.95 a week and giving it all to the swans; Len earned £100 a week and £72 of that was going to the swans. The couple lived on just £28 a week. All their other money went on grain, drugs, vets' bills, X-rays and petrol for the car. These were difficult days. Reflecting on them now Len calls them the black days. He knew that there was no going back, and that to give up rescuing the swans was out of the question, but there were moments also when he didn't know how to continue. 'One night I left work at 6.00 p.m. and got home at 3.30 in the morning after rescuing seven swans, two of which died. And we kept up that kind of pace for a long while. I used to feel myself falling asleep as I was driving the car; it was draining us both, physically and mentally.'

The black days continued and by October 1978, at the end of their first year, there were sixty-one swans in the garden. All that year the battle had been between the need for money to pay for the swan rescue and the time in which to carry it out. It was during one of Len's dark, anxious spells that he first met Marlon.

There is a bend in the River Bure which is a favourite spot of his. A willow stoops and touches the water, and Len calls it 'the place where the tree kisses the water'.

It's paradise just there. And if you get a little dinghy and sit very quietly in the reeds, under the tree, things unfold like a dream. It's where my water vole lives, and the coypu. You hear little plopping noises in the water and little shrill noises from the birds. It's pure paradise . . . until the humans wake up.

I was sitting in the reeds, in the mist, very early one morning, and from the mist materialized a white shape; it was a little female swan who at that time was living alone. She came out of the mist towards me, and as all swans do when they greet you, she moved her head up and down in jerky movements, and made a kind of snorting noise which means 'hello'. And I did it back and started to give her some bread which I always carry with me. And suddenly I heard a gentle hissing noise and another huge swan had appeared in the mist. She left me and went towards him. It was Marlon.

Suddenly I didn't matter any more, and the two of them completely forgot I was there. They swam towards each other and met in the middle of the river, it was a beautiful sight. The sun was just coming up and very, very slowly they touched each other chest to chest. Then they rubbed heads, then they did their greeting noises to each other, and then they decided, in a mysterious moment that no human could possibly understand, that they would bathe. Almost as if they'd been programmed by a computer they both started bathing, very slowly at first, then quicker and quicker. Heads under the water, water running over their back, and they laugh when they're happy, they open their beaks as wide as they can and you can see what fun they are having.

And then he gently took hold of her neck and mated with her. And I was there. I saw that beautiful moment, I shared it with them. And after, they bathed again and swam off together past me, down towards the speed limit sign where they were to build their nest and where the babies were born.

Len felt that he had been allowed into a secret part of the swans' life. Not exactly a reward for all the hard work he'd been putting in, but a reaffirmation that he was meant to be with swans, and to work with them. If he had any doubts, Marlon and his courtship of Pawline had dispelled them. How could Len leave what fate had obviously brought him to? The words of the Indian were in his mind now. Your destiny, he had been told, was with a big white bird. That magic moment on the river, in the mist, had been like an initiation ceremony. Len would struggle on. And he knew that Sheila was wholeheartedly behind him.

The reality, and the horror, of the situation was creeping upon them. The more they dealt with swans, and were called out to help those that were injured, the more they realized what a terrible plight the swans were in. But the Bakers themselves were getting into deep water.

There were times when they were called to a rescue but had no money for the petrol, and were forced to borrow. Every time a vet did an X-ray it cost them £12.50, and some swans needed many X-rays; one particular swan Len remembers had nine altogether. He had to buy drugs and he had to pay vets for treatments that he couldn't do himself. 'We got to a stage where we owed money to just about every vet in Norfolk. As soon as we ran up a bill with one we'd move on to another. I got to a position where there were no vets left, no vet would touch our swans because we hadn't paid our past bills. We were in trouble.'

Drastic situations call for drastic measures, so the Bakers sold the only things they had – their furniture and Sheila's jewellery. The jewellery raised £395. Her engagement ring was pawned for £40, and it was two years before they redeemed it. They visited as many second-hand shops as they could find with the aim of selling the furniture to the highest bidder. They were lucky. 'We did it, we raised over £2,000 and we paid off every vet. One had been waiting for nine minths for his money; the largest vet debt we had was £518. But we paid them all. When we came back to the house, it was comical really, there was just nothing in it.'

But fate, having brought them to this point, was to help them. A friend gave them some furniture, so they soon had basic tables and chairs again. Their activities were not pleasing the neighbours, however. The villagers didn't like the fact that visitors approaching Sparham were welcomed by the sight of many sickly swans. There were complaints about the smell, and grumbles that Len didn't cut his grass often enough. Even today when Sheila shops, no one but the shopkeepers speak to her. One morning Len looked out of his window and thought seven of the swans had died, for there were seven white lumps lying dormant in the garden. Inspection revealed them to be white bags full of rubbish, presumably chucked over the garden hedge by a disgruntled neighbour.

These somewhat basic human problems were the least of Len's worries. He had enough to contend with in the swan world, for the plight of the swans was becoming an everyday nightmare. Never a day passed without another little tragedy needing his attention. Every ounce of his energy, every ambition, every hope, was for the swans. To care for them, to give them a future, to mend their broken wings and damaged bodies was all he cared about.

Marlon and his lady Pawline had nested under the 7 knots speed limit sign on the river at Horning. Once the cygnets were hatched, like any male swan, Marlon did his lap of honour in the sky while his spouse cleared all the bits of broken shell out of the nest so as not to encourage rats. When they were forty-eight hours old the seven cygnets were nudged into the water by Marlon. They are not given any choice in the matter, for it is the father's duty to make sure they don't dally in the comfy nest too long, and a prod from his beak is enough to make any babe scurry along. The weak ones who find the ordeal a bit too much can always clamber on to their mother's back when he isn't looking.

Marlon spent most of those early days upside-down in the water pulling up reeds by the roots for the cygnets to eat. Pawline's task was to keep her eye on the seven bobbing little heads that seemed to disappear in the slightest ripple of water. There was much squeaking between mother and babies as she tried to keep them all in convoy, with Marlon intervening every now and again as if to say, 'Do what your mother tells you'.

But tragedy was to strike this little family. Two of the cygnets died before they were four days old: they got caught up in fishing line that had been left on the riverbank, and they drowned together. Marlon and Pawline attacked the bank; they couldn't understand why it had killed their babies. The third cygnet had lead-poisoning and a fish hook in its head. It died in Len's kitchen, aged four weeks. Three others died at five weeks from lead-poisoning. That left Marlon and Pawline with just one surviving cygnet.

I got called by a Cockney who was up here on holiday. He was a dockworker, a real cockles-and-whelks fella. He said, 'A bloody great swan here's got his kid in trouble.' The cygnet had a fish hook through its flesh and it was dragging a float and line. Now, Marlon is a warrior, I knew that. I knew he wouldn't just let me take his baby, and to be honest I was scared. I'd got to get that cygnet or it would die, so I had to act. But I'd got the assistance of this enormous Cockney, who was all hair and muscle, and he volunteered to hold a boat-hook between Marlon and the cygnet so that I could grab the baby. The last words I heard from the Cockney were, 'If he comes near you, son, he'll be straight in the oven.'

Not in favour of the sentiment but only too grateful for the help, Len was confident his Cockney friend wouldn't let him down. He grabbed at the cygnet and with luck on his side he caught it first go. He turned and ran, knowing that the most sensible thing was to get well away from Marlon. Several hundred yards away, and thinking he was safe, he stopped to look at the cygnet. He could hear people screaming and yelling at him but by the time he realized what was going on it was too late to take evasive action.

Suddenly I received a blow across my kidneys, I've never been hit so hard in all my life. I fell face down on the ground with the cygnet squeaking in my arms. Then I felt as though my back was being torn open by sheath-knives – it was Marlon standing on me and ripping me with his claws and hitting me with his wings. He wanted his baby back. He'd gone berserk. Every time I moved he hit me. I managed to crawl forward and stand up but he hit me across the back of my knees and I fell again.

Fortunately two men from a passing boat ran to Len's aid. They managed to fend off Marlon with an oar and eventually the irate swan went back into the water.

So there was Len, splattered with his own blood, shaking like a leaf with a bent cigarette still in his mouth, and the cygnet squeaking in his arms. He shouted to the Cockney, 'Fine bloody help you were.' The reply came back, 'You didn't tell me they could get out of the water.'

The little cygnet was taken away and tended. He had a hook in his thigh and couldn't use his left leg for four weeks. But he recovered, and was named Karl, and was later to nest just a few yards from where he himself had been born. We will hear more of him later.

Len scanned libraries and bookshops searching for books to help him learn about swans, but found little. It seemed that few people had studied or written about them. There were ornithological books on the migration patterns, nesting habits and mating of the birds, but nothing on diagnosing, treating and generally looking after them, apart from a fifteen-year-old veterinary dictionary which was of some assistance. He talked to eight vets in Norfolk who had never even touched a swan. The more Len searched for help the more apparent it became that there was none available. He was on his own. But he learned as he went. Commonsense and

35

care were his main guidelines, for every swan was a friend and was treated with love and tenderness.

The kitchen was the centre of operations at this time, with the early treatments being done on the draining-board. The purchase of a secondhand washing machine for Sheila was to improve things for the swans too. The machine was on wheels, and with the addition of a strong, flat surface laid across its top they now had an operating table that could be moved to wherever it was needed, and upon which the swans didn't slip and slide. They used it for two years.

For three years Len worked alone, with no professional guidance. He knew nothing of forceps or how to stitch wounds, but he managed. 'I was using carpenters' tools. I had a Stanley knife, some pliers and a needle and thread. As I'm not qualified some of the things I did were probably illegal, but when you've got a dying swan on a riverbank you've got no choice.'

But whenever deep surgery or amputations were needed he went to an expert, and eventually a friendly vet gave him some professional guidelines and a set of proper veterinary instruments. Len learned about metabolisms, blood cell structures and how to give injections, although it took some practice to master the latter.

I had a sick swan on the kitchen draining-board. Sheila was holding it still, and the needle went in like silk. And the swan just gazed up at me. Then Sheila said, 'Darling, there's liquid running down the window.' I'd gone under the surface of the swan's skin and out again. I'd injected the window! But I kept trying, and I perfected it after four or five goes.

Len was also reading the few books he had managed to get hold of and was learning about such absorbing subjects as parasites and fleas and why swans need them. He also found a shop in London that sold reconditioned surgical instruments and he bought some £300 worth of equipment. He spent hours cutting comfrey with the intention of using it for its healing properties on wounds, but results were very slow. On one occasion he bought a child's worming powder from Boots, blackcurrant flavour, but the swan didn't like it! But all the time he remembered what the Indians had told him: birds will show you how to heal them.

And they did. They know what's best for them. They taught me how to diagnose and how to judge how serious the problem was. And they taught me one other very important thing – when to stop working on them and give up. When to give them peace. Everything I know about swans I know because I live with them. It took me a long while to be able to spot a sick swan in a flock but I can do it now, and you gain all that from living with swans. You can't gain that from a book, it's a feeling.

Still the final decision had to be made: did he put his health and strength first and give up the swans, or did he do swan rescuing full time and give up working at the boatyard? He feels now that the swans made the decision for him. Their dignity and love had captured his heart, and Sheila's, and one spring morning in 1981, as they gazed out of their kitchen window on to the courtyard where the swans were struggling for survival, the answer to the situation became plain. Len was physically and mentally worn down, he couldn't keep up for ever the pace of just a few hours' sleep a night. The two of them agreed that he would stop working, which he did that May. Sheila continued working for a further six months, mainly to supply the money for the swans' grain, but she too was to stop before the year was out. In effect they had no reliable income. They threw themselves on the mercy and kindness of the general public: the Swan Rescue Service relied then, as it does now, totally on donations.

A friend of Swan Rescue, Eddie Bush, now one of the rescuing team, sold his motorbike for £500 which enabled Len to buy a dinghy to reach swans in previously inaccessible parts of the river. Two other swan friends, Paul and Sue Scheller, initiated fund-raising to buy the caravan that is now parked in the Bakers' garden and is their operating theatre. Many people have done many things, but we will come back to the generosity of the British people later. It is enough to say for the moment that without their generosity the Swan Rescue Service would not exist, which is ironic, since if it wasn't for the people it would not need to exist.

Since the birth of Swan Rescue in the autumn of 1977 Len Baker has gained a reputation. His work and research into the problems of swans, particularly those connected with lead-poisoning, is probably, on the grassroots level, the best in Britain. I know of no one else who lives with swans and studies them daily, or who has put so much energy into trying to publicize their plight.

Len Baker accuses the fishermen of Britain of ignoring facts and dismissing evidence that doesn't suit them. He has become embittered towards humanity in general for the torture and brutality that has been inflicted on the swans. He is angry with the various animal organizations which, he says, do nothing and waste much of the money they are given. He points a finger of scorn at the scientists who are working on various aspects of lead-poisoning, the main threat to swans, but are doing it slowly while taking fat salaries.

When it began Swan Rescue was mainly Norfolk based; now it is nation-wide. The team consists of twelve permanent volunteers who are always on call, plus various people around Britain who give help in their area as and when it is needed. 'I'll go anywhere to help a swan, there's no distance that I wouldn't travel. If a swan is in trouble I'll go to him,' says Len Baker.

Human Cruelty

And you will fly again
On mended wings,
Our thanks being your release
To freedom
And to fit back into
The scheme of things.

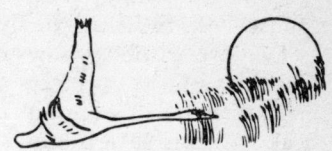

Horning, summer 1978
9.10 a.m. A woman hears a commotion in the trees which worries her. She can see that a swan is in trouble so she telephones Swan Rescue. At 9.40 a.m. Len is on the scene to witness the horrific sight of a swan crucified to a tree. Vandals had shot a crossbow bolt through its body, thereby pegging it to the tree. They had then held out its wings, one at a time, and shot bolts through those. The swan had been in agony for some thirty minutes. It died in Len's arms.

Norwich, summer 1979
Len and Sheila were called to Riverside Road in the centre of the city, by the river. Two children, a boy of seven and a girl of eleven, were holidaying with their parents on a boat. The sport, on this particular evening, was to stone a family of swans. Before Len got to the scene two of the cygnets were dead; he took two more home but they both died. Every bone in their bodies was broken. The parent swans weren't hurt, they just had their family wiped out. When Len tried to take up the issue with the children's parents, who had been on the boat watching television at the time, they replied: 'We are on holiday.'

Reedham, summer 1981
A woman reported to Swan Rescue that she had seen a red swan.

She was adamant that she hadn't imagined it. Len searched the stretch of river until 10 o'clock in the evening when the darkening light made him give up. At seven the next morning he was back on the scene and eventually he saw what looked like a red plastic shopping bag with something silver on it glinting in the sunlight. When Len got to the swan it had an eight-inch sheath-knife blade embedded in the top of its beak. There was blood everywhere, the swan's plumage was soaked in it. Len removed the knife and took the swan to a vet who mended the beak by wiring it together. At the time of writing, Beaky was recovering in Len's garden. As soon as he is fit he will be flying back to freedom.

Two eye-witnesses saw what happened to Beaky. A holiday-maker had lined up pieces of white bread along the back of his boat; when the swan put its head up to eat the man smashed at the beak with his sheath-knife. He had wanted a swan's beak as a souvenir of his holiday on the Broads. Len tried to prosecute this man but was unsuccessful.

These are just three cases with which Len has dealt. All are examples of the horror humans inflict on swans – the first and last deliberate perverted acts, the second an illustration of straight-forward lack of caring. Never a week, hardly ever a day, goes by without stories of this kind coming to Len's attention. Ipswich Docks, mentioned earlier, provide yet another example of the suffering caused to swans, this time by man's thoughtlessness. Years of busy activity in the docks had eliminated all natural food supply for the swans. Some sixty birds were living in a kind of swan hell. They were hungry, miserable, covered in oil, and many were dying. When Len visited the docks in March 1982 he couldn't believe his eyes.

I arrived in the early evening and can only describe the conditions for the swans as hell. If it wasn't for a very friendly group of nearby mill-workers the swans would have starved to death. The men let them eat their lunchtime sandwiches and the mill-owner lets them eat any grain that has spilled on to the floor.

The swans have evolved a kind of system for survival.

They know that everyday they are going to get covered in oil from the filthy water. I've never seen such a group of tatty, filthy swans. So they swim about a quarter of a mile to a discharge pipe that emits some kind of detergent from a nearby factory and they preen in that to try to get the oil from their lovely feathers. Swans hate being dirty, they are proud birds, but the preening means they are swallowing all that filth and making themselves ill.

They then have to search for food, and fortunately they have this nearby mill. They get out of the water, walk across a busy road, a railway line, across a lorry and car park, and up to the mill. At night they have nowhere to sleep so they shelter under the parked lorries; needless to say a few have been crushed.

They've been turned into beggars. They have to scrounge for food; in the docks they are the lowest of the low.

When Sheila and I went we didn't know which swan to pick up first, they were all in such a bad state. One particular swan couldn't walk, and obviously hadn't been able to for some weeks. He had gas-gangrene in both legs, they were rotten. He'd probably injured them and they had turned poisonous. Everyday this swan had to push himself along the concrete to get to the mill to eat. He'd completely worn away his tummy feathers and skin and about half-an-inch of his chest bone. He'd been in severe pain, wearing away his own body, and all because he was starving to death. His flesh was raw and he was rotting away. He was close to death.

The first thing I did, actually on the dockside, was to stick hypodermics into his legs to get the gas out. It puffed out like great lumps of foam. We cleaned the gunge, the filth and the maggots' eggs out of his undercarriage, dressed his wounds, and nursed him back to health.

He didn't have a name, he was just case 913. We released him a month later, a fit, healthy swan again.

Case 913 was not the only swan in a bad way. Others were scavenging around drainpipes to try to get fresh water. One couple had built their nest outside the friendly mill. Because they didn't have reeds and vegetation, the usual swan nesting materials, they had used pieces of plastic bags and fertilizer sacks. Len found old gaskets, bottle tops and bits of scrap in the nest. The swans, not to be beaten, were making do with what Ipswich

Docks had to offer. The female fortunately didn't have any cygnets, so the couple have been moved to a safer breeding place.

At the time of writing Len had removed forty-three swans from the docks. Some had died, the majority are either in their new homes or shortly to go to them.

On our first trip back from the docks we brought ten swans. We put them in the garden and gave them ten bowls of fresh, clean water. They put their beaks in them and it frightened them. We had to teach them to drink clean water and once they got the hang of it they loved it. Then they saw the food, and the grass – it was a miracle to them. They didn't have to beg any more. They were proud swans again.

The Royal Society for the Protection of Birds, at Len's request, contacted the dock authorities about the state of the docks and received assurances in reply that the authorities are very concerned about wild birds, and wildlife in general, on and around Ipswich Docks. The Harbour Master, in a letter dated 18 January 1982, wrote: 'Oil spillage and other forms of pollution are therefore guarded against as far as is reasonably practicable.' Reasonably practicable for whom, one may ask? Says Len:

It's the reply you get from all dock managers. How many boats they can get in and unload is the name of the game, the swans don't matter.

I've vowed I will take every swan away from those docks and find them new clean homes. If a healthy swan lands there I will take it away, and I'll never release any swans there. If the docks can't look after them, and just care a little, then I say swans shouldn't have to put up with it. Slowly I'll find them clean stretches of water where they can make proper swan homes.

Just down the coast from Ipswich is the attractive Essex village of Mistley. It has been famous for its swans for many centuries and has one of the country's oldest swanneries. It is said once to have been the home of over eight hundred of these beautiful birds, and still today a statue of a swan stands in the main street of the village. The statue could well become the only swan left, for once again the swans have become innocent victims of man. If Len's story was not so tragic it would be funny.

He first went to Mistley in 1980 to pick up three sick swans. They died, and a pathological report confirmed Len's suspicions that they had lead poisoning. But on that visit he was particularly worried by the behaviour of another swan that he had seen on a mudbank. It seemed as though it couldn't wake up. Other swans were swimming in the water around it, but this one was on the bank fast asleep. Len borrowed a dinghy and rowed over to the swan. It stood up, looked at him and fell over. A week later Len returned to Mistley and found seven other swans in much the same condition. They were drowsy, acting stupidly for swans, and a few of them were swimming about with their eyes closed. One was wobbling in the water, and it is in water that swans are at their most graceful. Len had met nothing like this before. He assumed that it was caused by a chemical leakage into the water, and if so it would be an almost impossible task to trace and to allocate blame.

Due to his other commitments back in Norfolk Len did not visit Mistley again until six months later. He was called out to attend another, obviously very ill, swan. It was taken back to their home and died; a post-mortem showed that the liver was significantly large and damaged, but the cause of death was unknown.

Another six months later Len returned again to Mistley. People had reported that the swans were looking funny. Accompanied by his brother Bob, he walked several miles along the coastline searching for clues as to what could be causing the drowsiness in the swans. The Mistley people were worried about their swans and the factory owners were happy to let Len on their land to look around. But Len and Bob could find nothing. They decided to go home, baffled by the mystery. As they were leaving they noticed a strange thing: nearly all the swans they had earlier seen dotted over the estuary had vanished.

There's no way in the world that nearly two hundred swans could have flown off without us hearing them. They'd vanished. We couldn't believe our eyes. We started looking for them, we were worried. We got out of the car and stood on the quayside and we both recognized a smell that had arrived around us. We knew it but we couldn't place it. Then we heard contented grunting noises and we looked over the quay edge, and there, about twenty feet down, were dozens of swans all lining up against the quay wall waiting their turn to eat the discharge that was being pumped into the water. It was discharge from a brewery. The reason Mistley's swans are dopey is because they are drunk. They are stoned out of their minds. And they obviously like it, because every day they queue and wait for the rumbling sound that comes from underneath the concrete because they know it is soon followed by the lovely stuff that makes them feel good.

Mistley's tipsy swans are probably unique, but although the story is amusing, it is sad too, for the swans are dying of drink. The enlarged and damaged liver of the earlier swan was probably caused by alcohol. Bob, who now helps Len with the swan rescuing, had a swan in his garden suffering from withdrawal symptoms. He needed his fix, but he was being weaned off his need. He was one of the lucky ones.

Marlon's only surviving cygnet, Karl, recovered from his fish hook injuries and after four and a half months Len put him back in the water about four miles away from Horning where he had been born. The next morning he was back at Horning. He didn't like the stretch of river he'd been given and wanted to be back at home. For three years he stayed in the area with the other non-breeders. He would fly off when it suited him, but he always reappeared at Horning and would seek out Len and say hello.

Then one day he returned with a ladyfriend and in triumph flew down low over Len's head. Len at the time was talking to a holidaymaker who was mopping up the deck of his boat. Karl swooped so low that the mop was dropped and the holidaymaker exclaimed: 'Blimmin' great seagulls you got up here!'

But Karl's courtship did not flourish. The lady didn't like him, or perhaps she didn't like Horning, who knows, but she didn't stay. So Karl was alone again. But after three years of bachelorhood he was obviously thinking about settling down, and Len was very happy about that. Then a pretty female swan came on the scene, and it was clear that they had fallen in love. Len wrote down his thoughts at the time.

They did their courting in the dyke and made love in the late afternoon, and Sheila and I were there on the riverbank while they performed their dance of magic. They would sit in the water facing each other, their beaks almost touching, and rub their long necks against each other, with eyes closed and in complete ecstasy. As we watched very discreetly, Karl slid on to her, holding her neck very gently with his beak and they rode on the water in contentment.

We both felt ashamed for watching and privileged for being able to. When the lovemaking was over she stood up on the water, neck straight up and her huge wings out. Karl did the same. Their chests touched, it looked as though it were one swan looking in a mirror.

Then they started to bathe, and continued bathing and preening for over an hour. We left them. As we drove away we glanced around one more time; they were swimming slowly away, towards the place where they were to make their home.

Karl and Karla nested on the same bank, only seven yards away from from where Marlon and Pawline had nested. Karla chose the spot and Karl helped by selecting pieces of twig and vegetation and passing them over his shoulder to the waiting Karla, who moulded them into the right nest shape with her big black feet. Using her body she would plop up and down to make the needed dish shape with her chest. Then she would go off in search of food and eat enormous amounts to sustain her through the important period ahead, for once the eggs are laid the female has to incubate them for up to thirty-five days. While Karla stocked up on food, Karl could be seen still at the nest, working away on the finishing touches.

They had five eggs, and every one hatched successfully. One morning, very early, the proud parents swam into the boatyard at Horning, one cygnet sheltering on its mother's back between her gently arched wings, the others swimming behind her. Karl was bringing up the rear. 'The beaks of the tiny cygnets looked as

45

though they were made of supple black leather and their squeaks sang of newness and hope as they travelled over the still water. What proud parents.' Then one day, only a short while later, a holidaymaker at the end of his stay on the Broads returned his cruiser to the boatyard. Something looking like a white bag was caught up in the propeller. It was Karl. The holidaymaker was greatly distressed; it had been a genuine accident, but yet another one to prove that boats pose a terrible threat to swans.

Now Len had a problem, for Karla was left with five cygnets only three weeks old. The family was very vulnerable. But Len had an idea. Back in the garden was a young male swan who had been trapped in a sluice gate at Bury St Edmunds and separated from his family. Would he take on the role of father? It was worth a try. So Len took him to the river and placed him in the water with Karla. 'If Karla hadn't liked him we'd have needed to get him out again quick, and that would have been very tricky! But all was okay. It was love at first sight, and he enjoyed being a dad. He took to the role straight away, no trouble.'

Needless to say, he became known as Karl II. This was the Bakers' first arranged marriage and a successful gamble, but in Len's words, it was a bitter-sweet experience.

Boats and swans do not mix. The action of boats damages riverbanks, in the process destroying the swans' food-supply of reeds. The boats themselves are a threat, for holidaymakers are not the most experienced of sailors, and do not always know how to take evasive action when necessary. Many a swan is caught between boat and bank; many a swan is hit, sometimes deliberately, by a passing oar or propeller, or by debris being thrown overboard.

The Broads is one of the most popular areas in Britain for boating holidays. Recent figures from the East Anglian Tourist Board show that there are some 2,300 boats available for weekly hire, about 1,000 on daily hire, plus about 9,000 owned privately. But the figures do not reflect the extensive use of these waters, for the boats actually supply about 250,000 people with week-long boating holidays and another 250,000 with day outings. It is estimated that the private launches and cruises are used by around 150,000 people.

On the Thames too, thousands of people take to the water. The Thames and Chiltern Tourist Board estimate that in a good holiday season of say thirty weeks, some 108,000 people will take to the river in boats.

Len Baker is unashamedly on the side of the swans, and of all water wildlife; he would like to see all the boats removed from our rivers and lakes. But he knows this will never happen, so he spends much of his time patching up swans after the inevitable accidents, and sometimes burying them.

At Coltishall village there is an old inn which fronts on to the river and is a very popular mooring place with holidaymakers. On summer days the area is full of chatter, transistor radios, dogs and children. Two dear friends of Len lived there, Loh and Grin. They have had two broods of cygnets. Loh is a warrior, Grin is a demure lady. Loh has been hooked seven times and shot once; Grin has been hooked four times. But just once Loh turned the tables and got his own back.

It was a Saturday morning in July. The police asked us to get to the river as quickly as possible; the swans weren't hurt, they said, but please get down there and have a look. We parked the car and ran down to the river's edge and in the water there was a sight to behold.

Loh was standing in the water, both wings in the attack position. In front of him was a battered fibreglass canoe and there were pieces of fibreglass floating in the water. Sheila and I watched, mesmerized. Loh cracked his mighty wing again at the canoe and a remaining thin piece of timber, its gunwhale, snapped like a match.

It was then we realized there were two people in the canoe, two very worried people! Sheila called to Loh and he stopped attacking. Sulkily he swam over to Sheila and she gave him a piece of his favourite brown bread, and he took the bread as gently as a lamb.

The two canoeists managed to get themselves and the remains of their canoe, on to the bank. They were fuming. They wanted to take action against the swans, against Swan Rescue, against anyone they could, for the damage that had been caused to their boat. They were shouting all sorts of abuse. By now a crowd had gathered, cameras were clicking, and knowledgeable parents were telling startled children how a swan can break a man's arm, leg, neck and back. Loh, still with Sheila, was quietly eating his brown bread.

They noticed a timid old lady trying to make herself heard over the general hubbub. She was coughing nervously, trying to get a word in among the chaos all round them. Len and Sheila asked the old lady what she had seen. She pointed an accusing finger at one of the canoeists and said she had seen him hit the swans' nest with an oar. His guilty look confirmed the absence of a denial. 'I saw him,' insisted the little old lady. Loh had also seen him, and Loh did not approve!

Loh and Grin still live on that stretch of river. When the Bakers go to visit them, the swans come out of the water to greet them.

When the hurt becomes too much and the day is dark, and things begin to lose their reason, and the fight becomes too hard, we go to the river and we talk to Loh and Grin. They come out of the water and on to their preening place and they waddle up the sloping bank towards us. We go down on our haunches to their height. Loh is fascinated by the press-stud on the collar of my jacket. He pecks at it and quizzically turns his head from side to side. Grin stays just behind Loh and gently takes bread from Sheila's hand. A peace exists. Life becomes tolerable again.

Not long after the canoe incident Swan Rescue was telephoned by a holidaymaker who said she had seen a swan being towed by a boat. She told them that she was staying at Stokesby, near Yarmouth, on the Broads, but not wanting to become involved any further she rang off. Len and Sheila searched nearly the whole of that day, but could find no swan in distress. The next day, a Sunday, Len received a further call. Another holidaymaker said he had seen a swan with a rope around its neck, in the reeds, unable to move. The location? Stokesby. Back Len went and this time he found the swan. It had a dislocated vertebra, and died. Investigations revealed that someone had lassoed the swan and towed it at speed for about half an hour. Around this time Len encountered four cases of swans being lassoed and towed.

Another young swan caused a mystery, for it wouldn't move or stand up although there appeared to be nothing wrong with it. This was confirmed by an X-ray and a vet's examination; there were some feathers missing around its neck, but apart from that it was perfectly sound. But it just used to sit, absolutely still, all day long. Sheila bathed it and nursed it, stroked its head and talked to it, but to no avail. One day they returned from a rescue to find that the little swan, which was eighteen months old, had died. A post-mortem confirmed that there had been nothing wrong with it.

A few days later a woman telephoned, inquiring about the swan. So upset was she to hear it had died that she ventured to tell what she had seen. Two boys on a motorbike had tied a rope around the swan's neck and towed it at speed round and round a field. This elderly lady had called to them to stop but they had sworn at her and threatened her. Understandably she had been too frightened to intervene.

The little swan, obviously in deep shock, had just surrendered its will to live. The ordeal had been too much for it.

The inhumanity of man is probably what has hurt Len most during his years with the swans. He remembers vividly the night that he didn't get to the vet in time with one very badly injured swan. It had lost a leg and left wing when it was cut by a boat propeller. He realized the bird couldn't be saved, but it died in his arms before the vet was able to give it a releasing injection. Onlookers later told Len that the man responsible had been drinking. He turned to the crowd that had gathered and lifting his glass in toasting fashion announced, 'That's another one out of the way.'

Swans like to fly at dawn and dusk. Not that you are likely to see flocks of them any more, but they can be spotted in twos and threes. Unfortunately, because of the deceptive light, these two times of day are the most dangerous for them to be flying.

To a swan dancing among the clouds and playing hide-and-seek over the tree tops, a wet road must so easily look like an inviting river on which to rest. And all too often that seems to be what a swan does think, and it ends up with broken ribs or broken legs, and always in a severe state of shock. Sometimes they are killed outright.

When swans are coming into land, power cables too present a tremendous hazard. In one year alone Len had forty-nine power cable fatalities, plus many birds severely injured. The cables that criss-cross this country range from 11,000 to 400,000 volts. A swan with its huge wing span can easily hit two cables, which means that it dies immediately; or it can hit one cable and something else, say a tree, and again that means instant death. These are the lucky ones, for they know nothing of what has happened to them. But others don't die. They get severe burns across their faces and chests, or their legs are completely severed. They fall to the ground stunned, in pain, sometimes unconscious. Many die in a lonely corner of a field, unnoticed and unattended.

Swan Rescue is frequently called out to these tragedies, for sometimes the accident damages the electricity supply, which at least brings attention to the fact that a cable has been hit by something, very often a swan.

This was what had happened at Haddiscoe in Norfolk, when a six-month-old cygnet flew into, and damaged, a cable. Unfortunately for this particular cygnet that was just the first stage of a series of misfortunes. The cable shattered its left wing in three places and it was bleeding badly. The swan was also burned across the chest. It dropped to the ground and after a while managed to start walking. After about three-quarters of a mile it was hit by a car; the driver didn't stop. The struggling cygnet managed to cross a road and take refuge in a field, only to be harassed by bullocks. Little Haddiscoe, as this little warrior was named, is still in Len's garden. He had to have his left wing amputated, and he still limps from his leg injuries. He'll never know freedom again, but at least he is safe where he is.

'Some people think it is cruel to keep alive a swan with only one wing. That's nonsense. He may mate with another swan with one wing one day and they may have many healthy cygnets. That's beautiful.' Apparently Little Haddiscoe has been wooing a female swan which is convalescing in Len's garden. Primrose had only got one wing, but she's a very pretty swan. She is playing hard to get at the moment, but Len has great hopes.

*   *   *

Swans are remarkably fastidious birds when it comes to personal hygiene. They cannot abide being dirty, and being soaked in oil is as damaging to their psyche as it is to their pride. Unfortunately it is pride that can kill them, for the first thing they do when their feathers become dirty is to preen. If what they are trying to remove is oil, it can kill them. They will preen for hours – pointlessly of course, but they don't know that. Nor do they know that they are poisoning themselves in the process, for they are taking the oil into their systems.

The first thing Len does with oil-polluted swans is give them tablets to nullify the toxicity. He watches their faces, and once he is sure the toxicity is out of their systems he starts attemping to get the oil from their feathers. 'We've tried every known washing-up liquid on the market. We can't use detergent because that can kill them too. The posh liquids that are kind to hands are next to useless when it comes to feathers. By trial and error we've discovered that the Woolworth and Co-op washing-up liquids are best for swans.' During one oil-soaked season the Bakers had ten swans pass through their bathroom in two days.

Three particular swans that came to Len because they were saturated with oil taught him an invaluable lesson. Swan Rescue had been called to Birmingham because someone had poured gallons of diesel oil into a pond in which some swans lived. Three live birds were taken to the Bakers' home, plus two dead birds whose post-mortem established that they had died from ingesting diesel oil. Len put the three live swans in a pen on their own, just in case they had any other disease which might spread to his other swans. He watched this trio daily, and then a curious thing happened.

They started going bald, just from the neck up, nowhere else. I telephoned various expert contacts of mine but no one could understand why they should go bald just from the neck up. I sat and watched them for hours, it was a phenomenon I just couldn't understand. They looked so funny. Imagine a perfectly normal swan body, a bald neck and a tiny tuft on the top of the head.

But suddenly Len had an idea, and enquiries made at Esso

confirmed his suspicion.

There's something in diesel that kills insects. All the thousands of fleas that always live on a swan were now living on a diesel-soaked swan. It was killing them. They wanted to get off the swan so they had all fled to the highest point, the swan's head. Thousands of them had all congregated at the same place and were eating the swans' feathers away, that's why the three of them had gone bald.

For six weeks Len treated the swans, three times a day, with flea powder. They soon regained their beautiful plumage and their oil treatment also completed, the three of them were released at Lowestoft.

Len observes:

Feather condition of a swan is vital for waterproofing. It has been believed for years that a swan waterproofs himself with oil from his preen gland, using his beak to put the oil on to his plumage. This is not so. The only thing that makes a swan waterproof is the mechanical properties of the feathers. If the feathers are not perfect the bird is not waterproof, so obviously oil is a terrible threat to them.

It has also been believed that cygnets become waterproofed by their mother transferring her preen gland oil to them. Len says this is also wrong. When a cygnet is just a few days old, and before it goes into the water, it will rub itself under its mother's body and thus produce static electricity. This makes the down stand out and creates buoyancy when the cygnet is in the water. This was one of Lady Wednesday's tasks as surrogate mother to the 118 orphaned cygnets in her care. So what does Len do with the cygnets now that Lady Wednesday has died? 'We rub their bodies very quickly with a silk cloth and that has the same effect. It only has to be done once a day for the first few days. They very quickly learn to preen themselves and get their own down the way it is needed. They're born knowing all the secrets.'

Blood-soaked plumage does not present a problem. Once the emergency treatment has been given the swan gets a hot bath, and ordinary soap and water soon bring the feathers back to the spotless white that they should be.

Not everything comes off so easily, however. Len received a phone call from someone saying they had seen a brown swan. Yes, Len informed them, swans are brownish for the first eighteen months of their life. The caller insisted that this particular swan had been white in the morning, but was brown in the afternoon. Was it a different swan, Len wondered? No, the caller was adamant. It had a distinctive scar on its beak: it was definitely the same swan. Len went to the scene and searched for some time. Suddenly he saw it, sitting in the middle of the river – a shiny brown swan that looked as if it were made of wood.

It wouldn't come to us, but its eyes were moving. We got a dinghy and went out to it. It was in a bad way, but we managed to lift it gently aboard. And Sheila kept saying she knew the smell but couldn't place it.

They asked around and discovered what had happened.

A family was on holiday on a boat moored at this spot. The parents had gone into Yarmouth leaving five children, aged from two to thirteen, alone on board. They became bored and started cooking for fun. They found a large tin of golden syrup which they boiled in a saucepan. They enticed the swan to the boat with bread and them poured the hot syrup over him.

The swan was badly burned and very stunned. Len had to cut off nearly all its feathers, for there was no other way of dealing with the sticky mess. He also dressed the wounds. The swan lived and was later released, still looking a little tatty because not all his feathers grew again.

Happily, Len does sometimes receive false alarms. He was contacted by a local man who introduced himself as a teacher of birdwatching. He had got one quick question to ask Len: how do you get paint off a swan? Len explained that it depended on what kind of paint it was. Water-based paint was no real problem; gloss paint, on the other hand, was. The caller didn't know what kind of paint it was. He'd seen an orange swan through his binoculars and was able to tell Len exactly where it had landed. For nearly three hours Len and Sheila searched for the orange swan, until suddenly Sheila burst out laughing. 'What's the matter?' asked Len. 'I'm not going to scrub that,' said Sheila, 'it's a flamingo!'

Apparently it had escaped from a local zoo and as far as Len knows still lives happily, in the wild, in Norfolk.

It is tragic but nevertheless true that just about everything man does is a threat to swans. Cars run over them, boats crush them, power cables kill them, even our roads when wet deceive them. And how are they to know that railway lines are dangerous places to be near? Len recalls what he named the 'Reedham Railway Rescue'.

We were called by British Rail and asked to go to Reedham, near Yarmouth, where a train had hit a family of swans. We walked half a mile along the railway line and could find nothing. Then we found some feathers and thought the worst. Sheila suddenly shouts and starts to run, she has spotted something moving in between the railway lines and a train is coming. It is a tiny cygnet, a ball of fluff. Stay still, for God's sake stay still. Sheila puts her hands over her eyes and waits. The train thunders past. The cygnet is still there, we run and pick it up. It is okay apart from a minute chip out of the tip of its little black beak. Sheila puts the tiny bundle down the front of her jacket. I find another baby by the side of the track; it is dead, and still warm. I lay it gently on the grassy bank and go in search of the rest of the family. I cross the track and search the marsh. There, in a narrow dyke is the pen. She has black grease marks on her neck but seems unharmed. But where is the cob?

I search the marsh but no swan. It is so quiet, the only sound being my own feet squelching in the mud. I turn to cross another dyke and suddenly from the reeds comes a very big, very angry swan. He is coming towards me with his wings in the attack position. I do the same and, hissing at each other, we stand face to face. I wave my arms up and down – I am now a bigger swan than he is. He calms down, to my relief. He waddles quickly towards the dyke; there is obviously nothing wrong with him. He swims like fury towards his remaining family, they meet and all four are now safe.

Sheila and I stay for a while and watch the family and wonder. They are all eating now. Are they in ignorance of the tragedy or is it an acceptance? Have they forgotten already? Are they aware they were once six and now they are only four? We will never know. We head back to the car, the hurt cygnet still safe and warm inside Sheila's jacket. He didn't live long, he died peacefully at our home. He would never know the magic of flight or the freedom in the sky, but moments like this make Sheila and I more determined than ever to make sure that other swans do.

After trains and boats, planes must inevitably follow, although they are an infrequent hazard. The only occasion on which Swan Rescue was called in to save swans from aircraft turned out to be a very poignant one.

A man working at RAF Coltishall, where Len himself had once been based, telephoned to ask if Len could help with a problem. David Bullock, a winch operator with 202 Helicopter Rescue Squadron, was worried about a family of swans that had made their home in a pond near a runway used by the RAF's Jaguar aircraft. He was concerned for the swans, but obviously too for the safety of the pilots and aircraft. They were a hazard to each other. Could Len look into it? Of course he could, and did.

The swan parents had seven three-week-old cygnets and they all seemed very content in their pond, happily accepting the aircraft screeching over them.

They just looked up at the planes with envy, as if to say 'one day perhaps we'll fly like that'. But they had to be moved, they were going to get killed, something had to be done with them. Now I had a problem for there were nine of them. I could see the water was only a few feet deep but I couldn't judge how deep the mud was. I could see dangers lurking.

The lads of 202 Squadron agreed to don their survival kits and go into the water with Len. Their task would be to grab a cygnet each; Len would take care of the adult swans. A great plan, but the swans weren't playing! The task was to prove more difficult than these strong, burly men could ever have imagined, for the cygnets screeched and scurried away at the sight of them.

Len explained to David Bullock that there was every possibility that the female might attack on seeing him and his men going for her babies. If she did, they should raise their arms like wings and hiss aggressively. The inevitable happened: the female went for David, who waved his arms very gently and hissed very politely. The female kept coming. 'Hiss!' shouted Len. David hissed again, this time slightly more loudly, but he wasn't fooling the lady. She knew David was no swan! Danger was in sight and David scampered from the pond, chased by the female.

Eventually Len grabbed the mother, and David and his men went back into the pond to retrieve the cygnets. It took seven men six long hours to catch seven tiny cygnets. Apparently when colleagues ask them about it, they deny the incident!

Not long after that event a plane crashed in the North Sea and David Bullock's team was called out to rescue the pilot. David, the winch man, was lowered into the water. He managed to gather up the struggling American pilot but as they were being lifted back to safety the winch broke. Both men drowned. David was awarded the George Medal for bravery, an award seldom made posthumously.

In a private lake four miles from RAF Coltishall the family of swans now lives in safety. When Len and Sheila took them to their new home they released the cygnets one by one into the water while the father stood on the bank and waited. When every one of his seven babies was out of the box, the family did their exploratory lap of the lake, father in front followed by the cygnets, mother bringing up the rear.

One icy winter's morning the cleaning ladies on the boats at Horning boatyard asked Len if he could move Marlon. Apparently the huge swan was sitting by the steps which they had to pass and they were frightened of him. Len obliged and coaxed Marlon back into the river, thinking at the time that Marlon didn't look too well. The next day Marlon was out of the water again, sitting on his own on the opposite side of the bank to his nesting place. Len was worried. He knew that this desire to be alone was the sign of a sick swan, so he took Marlon to a local vet.

The vet was out on calls and the receptionist, rather hesitantly, allowed Len to persuade her that he should leave Marlon until the vet returned. A few hours later Len received a call from the vet, a very angry one: 'Come and get this bloody swan out of my surgery.' Len went immediately and on opening the door discovered chaos. 'I've never seen a mess like it. It looked as though a bomb had hit it. The tables were upside down, papers and magazines were everywhere, swan's droppings were all over the floor, even running down the chairs.' Marlon had been left in a blanket secured with sticky tape, but he'd broken out. He clearly didn't like this surgery!

Len offered to clear up, but his offer was rejected. 'Just get yourself and your swan out.'

'But he's ill,' pleaded Len.

'Out!' shouted the vet. 'Out!'

A somewhat puzzled Len lifted the now docile Marlon into his car and took him back to the river, thinking that he couldn't be so ill if he was able to create such havoc.

Some ten days later Len was with three friends when Marlon turned into the boatyard and swam straight towards him. He got out of the water and greeted Len, opening his wings and hissing. He then got back into the water, swam over to his nest, climbed on to it and died. One of the friends standing with Len remarked that never in the twenty-seven years he had worked on the river had he seen a swan thank a human before.

The cause of Marlon's death was at that time a mystery to Len. Pawline had been killed by a crossbow bolt two days before, and knowing how much swans love each other Len half wondered if Marlon had died of a broken heart.

He was to discover later that in fact Marlon was seriously ill from lead-poisoning, and if he had known then what he knows now he might well have been able to save Marlon's life. 'Mind you, he was lost without Pawline. He was ill, but losing her was the last straw, it was as though his will to live had gone.'

Lead

It is not the darkness
That worries me.
It is the journey to it.

A lorry driver appeared one morning in the busy surgery of a London vet. A little out of breath, he had obviously been hurrying. Well, he had some vital news. 'Do you know anything about swans?' he asked the vet. The vet did not know a lot, but offered his services if the man cared to take the sick swan to him.

'He's already dead,' announced the lorry driver.

The vet pointed out that in that case there was little he could do to help.

'But you don't understand,' replied the man with urgency, 'it was lead that killed it and I thought you vets wanted to know about the dangerous effects of lead on swans.'

'You know about swans then,' said the vet. 'You've examined the bird?'

'No.'

'Then how do you know it's lead that killed it?'

'Because,' replied a now somewhat impatient lorry driver. 'I saw it. It rolled off the back of the lorry and squashed the bloody swan. It killed it outright.'

This story, one of the more amusing to come Len's way, is true. At least it indicates that the general public is becoming more and more aware of the fact that lead and swans do not mix, even if this man had got the wrong end of the stick.

The lead-poisoning controversy has been going on for many years. Anglers, who for a long time vehemently denied that their digested lead weights kill swans, as well as other water birds, now have to accept this as a fact. But they still claim that their sport is no worse a threat to swans than power cables or stone-throwing children.

Sadly this is not true. Lead-poisoning is the greatest single threat to swans and their future survival, and it is anglers who are mainly responsible for the lead. The charge against anglers is a simple one: that they leave riverbanks and reed areas where they fish littered with the lead that they use to weight their lines. Sometimes the lead weights fall off the lines, sometimes they are deliberately discarded, sometimes they are accidentally dropped.

Len Baker accuses the anglers of making the rivers of our country a death-trap for swans. He says that if there were no fishing his Swans Rescue Service would only have to do a couple of hours' work a week. For the threat posed to swans by the anglers is not only that of lead-poisoning, it also includes the danger of hooks and line. But let us look first at the problem of lead-poisoning, for it is the most lethal.

In the early days of setting up Swan Rescue, Len, like most other people in Britain at that time, knew next to nothing of the dangers of lead-poisoning to swans. He was aware that many of the swans he came across had funny necks. Sometimes their necks lay across their backs, limp and useless, and usually these birds died. They were a mystery to Len, who thought that the condition must be due to a muscular disease. But these swans had other things in common. Their faeces were a horrible khaki diarrhoea which stained their tail feathers, their tongues were the same greeny-blackish colour, and they had very bad breath. Len recalls: 'We were getting birds in this condition very frequently, sometimes as many as two or three a week, and they were all dying. We had so many dead swans we didn't know what to do with them.'

At Sutton Bonnington, near Loughborough, there is a Ministry of Agriculture, Fisheries and Food (MAFF) veterinary investigation centre which currently handles hundreds of swan corpses, or the vital organs of dead swans. Today in this establishment the discovery of lead-poisoning as the cause of death in swans is commonplace. In the early seventies it was not.

Alan Hunt, a clinical biochemist at the centre, says that their first analysis of lead-poisoning in a swan was in 1973; it was probably the first in Britain. The swan had been taken to the centre by the RSPCA. Some ten swans had died in a short period of time and the Society couldn't keep putting the somewhat alarming rate of death down to old age, so they wanted a post-mortem. The swan was shown to have lead, which worried Alan Hunt, and he asked the RSPCA to continue sending him their dead swans. This they did, and word soon spread that Sutton Bonnington, and gradually other MAFF establishments, were interested in studying the effect of lead on swans.

The corpses of swans from the Midlands were usually sent directly to Sutton Bonnington; otherwise parts of the swans, kidneys, livers, blood and bones, were sent from all parts of Britain. Alan Hunt's records show case entries ranging from Cornwall to northern Scotland.

In the first year, 1973, 29 swans were received by Alan Hunt; 18 were confirmed lead deaths (62.1 per cent). The numbers sent grew slowly during the seventies: in 1975 he received 40 swans, of which 30 were lead victims (75 per cent); in 1979, of 49 swans, 49 per cent had died from lead.

As the seventies came to their close the whole question of the lead threat to swans was receiving more publicity. Members of the public were encouraged to take dead swans to the authorities, and to report sickly-looking swans to animal welfare groups. In 1980 the number of swans Alan Hunt received shot up to 149, some 57 of these (38.3 per cent) having died from lead. In 1981, of 251 dead swans 41 per cent had died from lead; in 1982, he dealt with 277 swans, 41.5 per cent of which were confirmed lead victims. By the end of 1982, Alan Hunt, since 1973, has investigated a total of 976 swan deaths, of which 459 were found to have lead, representing 47 per cent of all deaths.

Of all the lead-poisoned swans analysed the average amount of split shot in their gizzards was nine pieces; the most Alan Hunt has seen in one swan is forty-four.

Meanwhile, Len was doing his bit in Norfolk. At £10 plus VAT a time he could not at first afford the luxury of getting post-mortems on all his swans, and many ended up with a 'death unknown' tag. But at the end of 1979 he was asked by the Ministry of Agriculture to start submitting his dead swans to them for investigation. Since then his swans have gone either to

MAFF or to the Institute of Terrestrial Ecology, and by the end of 1982 a total of 799 had been given post-mortems, 583 of which were lead victims. He has kept all the post-mortem reports, some of which make gruesome reading.

Given that lead is a toxic substance and shouldn't be in our environment at all, the fact remains that both humans and animals are suffering from it. Mute swans, it would seem, have a good resilience to it and it takes quite a high dose to kill them. It is generally accepted that a lethal level of lead in the kidney of a mute swan is about 250 parts per million. Some of Len's post-mortem reports are therefore quite astounding. A four-year-old swan that died in June 1982 was found to have 954 parts per million in its kidney; eight pieces of anglers' split shot were found in its body. Many other swans examined have had similar high levels of lead, and many too have been found to have anglers' lead in them.

In those early days of Swan Rescue many of Len's cures were more by luck than judgement. Commonsense told him and Sheila that one answer was to try to make the lead pass through the swan's body, so they would both spend many hours massaging the swans to try to keep movement going. Sometimes they were successful, often they weren't.

Bernie Legbiter was one of the lucky ones. When he was found he was in a bad way. His neck was lying right across his back, he couldn't see where he was going, and the only thing standing up was his beak. He had lost his bodily co-ordination, but still apparently had enough sense to know that if he waited for a passing boat to create a wash the waves would send him sailing to the riverbank. He could bounce a few times against the bank until he stopped, and there he would wait until, with luck, somebody threw him some food. Len was called and Bernie was taken home for treatment, but he was nearly dead.

'We started treatment on him immediately. We force-fed him grit and we gave him Complan and glucose by tube. We sat up with him all night and he made it till morning. We couldn't believe it, he even looked a tiny bit better.'

An X-ray showed that Bernie had four pieces of lead in him, which confirmed that he was suffering from lead-poisoning. For six weeks Sheila and Len worked on Bernie, massaging and nursing him. They were rewarded: the four pieces of lead passed through Bernie's system and today he still lives on a local river. He was given the name Legbiter because he liked to snap at people's ankles – as with humans, lead in the system tends to make for aggression!

Why do swans get lead-poisoning? Swans are vegetarians and live mainly on reeds. They eat other things as well, such as bread, cabbages and green vegetation of various kinds, but reeds are their favourite diet. When they eat they up-end in the water; their necks go down a long way and they pick up vegetation and riverbank deposits, which of course contain things other than food. The split shot that anglers use as weights are much the same size as the pieces of grit that the swans need for digestion, so they swallow them and the poisoning begins.

For a long time fishermen have denied that they present this hazard to water fowl, but the case against them is now conclusive. In 1981 the Nature Conservancy Council issued a report entitled 'Lead-poisoning in Swans', which stated that there is no doubt swans are dying as a result of lead-poisoning due to ingestion of fishing weights, especially split lead shot. The report also carried post-mortem data on swans from various parts of England. On the River Trent in the nine years up to 1981 some 118 swans were examined; 106 had died from lead-poisoning, representing an average death-rate from lead over the nine years of 90 per cent. At Stratford-upon-Avon in the eight years leading up to 1981, 70 swans were examined; 54 had died from lead, an average annual death-rate of 77 per cent. On the River Thames in the three years up to 1981, 72 swans were examined; 54 had died from lead, an average of 75 per cent a year.

The report went on to say: 'the population [of swans] on the River Thames has declined substantially since the 1960s . . . The severity of the problem increases downstream towards London with as many as 85 per cent of the birds examined below Windsor dying from lead-poisoning.'

Research was done into other causes of swan deaths, including collisions, internal injuries, infections, shooting and oil, but lead-poisoning emerged as the largest single threat. Out of 288 swans examined across the country 113 died from lead; 79 from collisions; 29 from internal injuries; 30 from infection; 16 were shot or killed; 2 died from oil; 19 had no diagnosis.

The high figure for collisions is also significant, for lead-poisoning impairs vision and co-ordination which possibly contributes to collisions. The 29 that died from internal injuries might well have swallowed fish hooks or fishing lines, the other threats presented by anglers which we shall look at later.

Len Baker claims that even if fishing were stopped immediately in Britain there would still be enough lead left in rivers and on banks to wipe out all remaining swans. This might be seen by some as over-dramatic, but split shot has been in use for at least 150 years, and some of our riverbanks are littered with it. Between June 1978 and March 1979 junior members of the Royal Society for the Protection of Birds found 3,000 pieces of split lead shot on riverbanks; they also recovered over six miles of discarded fishing line. The thirty miles of riverbanks covered give an average per mile of 86 pieces of split shot, seven hooks and 808 feet of line. No doubt much more went undetected, for split shot is pea-sized and difficult to find in grassy areas and undergrowth.

Alan Hunt's work on swan deaths at Sutton Bonnington veterinary investigation centre, and the fact that he was in at the beginning of the lead threat discoveries, has developed in him a personal involvement with the welfare of swans. He told me that on one occasion he and a friend, walking along the concrete embankment of the River Trent in Nottingham, noticed a lot of anglers' split shot. They began picking it up, and after a while they had collected 1,000 pieces – enough, he says, to have killed about 200 swans. On another occasion he alone, in one hour, picked up 2,000 pieces of lead shot from the Nottingham embankment.

Lead on concrete is just as bad as in reeds, for the river swans of Britain have, unfortunately, become tame enough to walk up to busy populated areas and take bread that is thrown to them, often gulping down lead bits too. So many stretches of our town and city riverbanks are now covered in concrete that the lead sits there, waiting to be eaten; at least in rural areas there is a chance of the lead disappearing deep into the mud or being trodden into the ground by passers-by. This was proven by some East Midland schoolchildren who were set the task of washing out riverside soil. Using a wire grid one foot square the children were told to scoop up the earth to a depth of one inch beneath their grids. They then washed this in river water and counted how many pieces of lead shot they found. The average was in the region of four per square foot of earth, the maximum was twenty-five.

It is estimated that 250 tons of lead is turned into fishing weights every year by the tackle manufacturers. That is the equivalent of two pieces of shot per foot per year along all lowland rivers and canals. On those statistics the swans would seem to stand little chance. This is what Len Baker feels, for he sees his swans and their cygnets dying with heart-breaking regularity from lead-poisoning. Although the Nature Conservancy Council report did not appear to consider East Anglia to be an area with a particularly acute lead problem, the centres of Stratford-upon-Avon, Reading and Nottingham were seen to be faring far worse than most.

The National Anglers' Council refutes the NCC report figure of 250 tons of lead a year, although that figure was supplied by the tackle manufacturers. The NAC says the figure is nearer 50 tons. It does not accept either that all the split lead gets dropped on the ground. It is indisputable, however, that the highest number of deaths from lead-poisoning occur between June and September, coinciding with the start of the coarse fishing season in June, and the holiday season when the two-weeks-a-year fishermen come on the scene.

There are two other possible causes of metallic lead-poisoning in swans, other than fishing lead. Small granules of lead shot used in boatyards for shot-blasting the keels and sides of dry-docked boats may contaminate the immediate area of the boatyard. The Nature Conservancy Council report states that there is no evidence of swans ingesting this shot-blasting lead. Secondly, swans have been known to ingest shotgun pellets. The NCC report states that in post-mortems on 299 swans between 1973 and 1980 five birds had gun shot in them. Len Baker has also witnessed swan deaths from gun shot lead.

Death from lead-poisoning is a long, slow agony for the swan. Depending on the bird's age and how much lead it has swallowed, death can take up to six weeks.

Swans, like all birds, have no teeth, so they take in a lot of grit

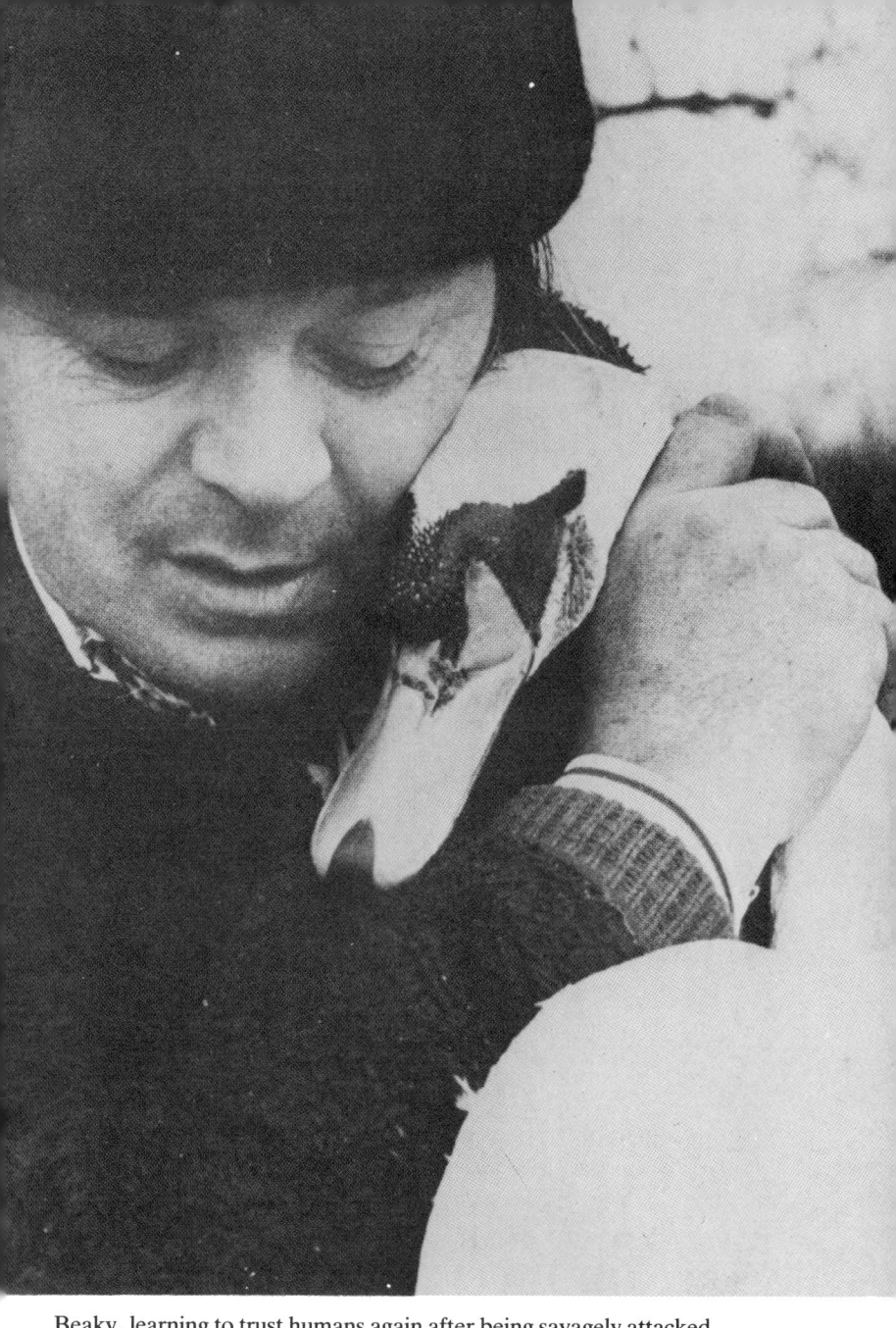

Beaky, learning to trust humans again after being savagely attacked.
The scar on his beak shows where the sheath knife plunged into him.

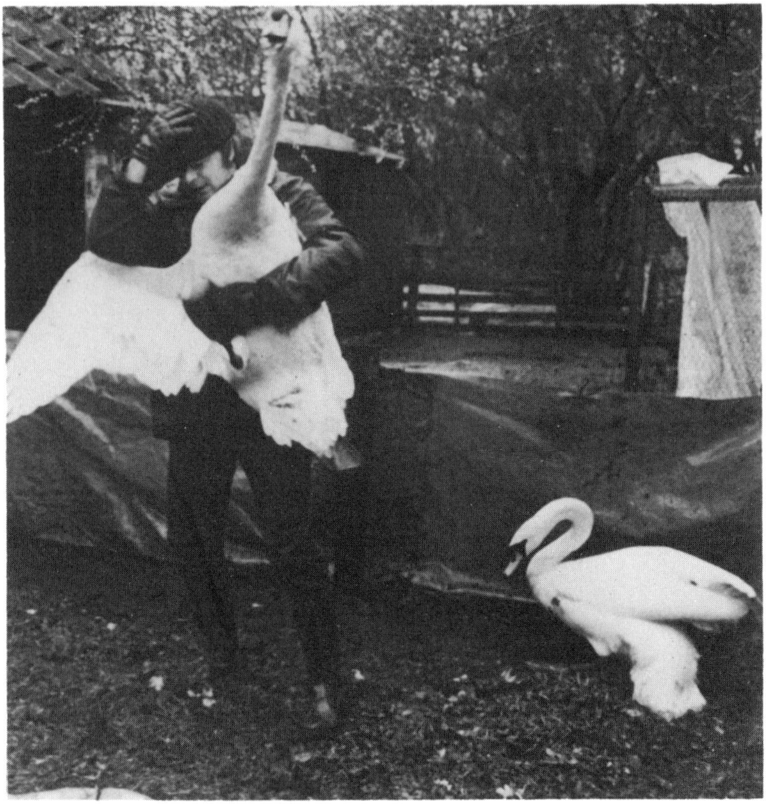

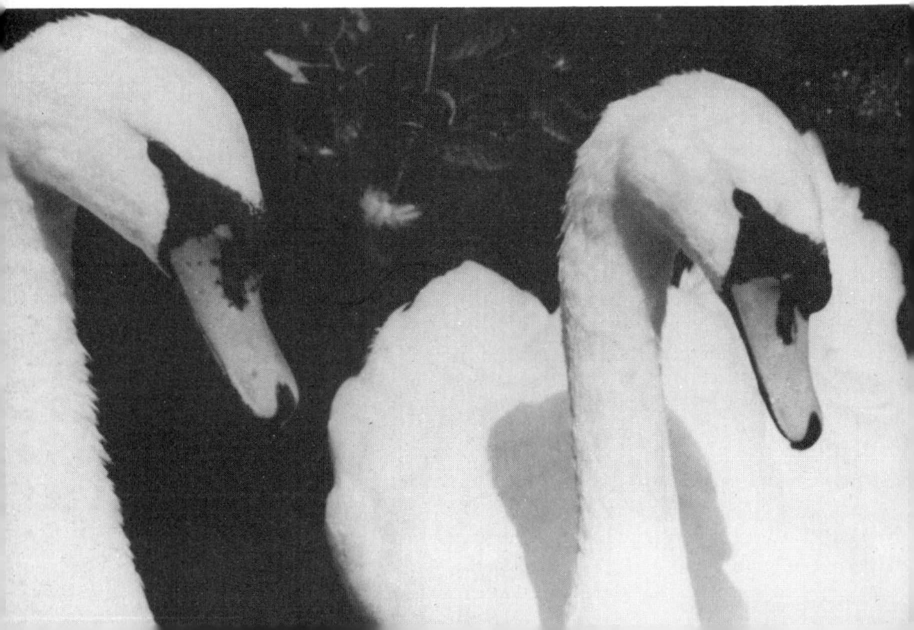

Opposite Above:
Paulette and Paul, another special couple, for she was Marlon's grandaughter. Two days after being released, Paul *(in Len's arms)* hit a power cable and was killed. Paulette died of heartbreak four weeks later and is buried in Len's garden. *(Photo by Lynda Freebrey)*

Opposite Below:
Zorba and Zoretta were to become Len's and Sheila's close friends, even though Len lost four teeth when Zorba attacked him.

Above:
Len always dreamed of giving the swans a safe haven of their own and he has succeeded with Marlon Land. *(Photo by Paul Felix)*

Len's surgery is now a far cry from the early days when operations were performed on top of the washing machine. Here a diesel-soaked swan from Malden, Essex is examined. It will be a year before the swan regains its white plumage. *(Photo by Paul Felix)*

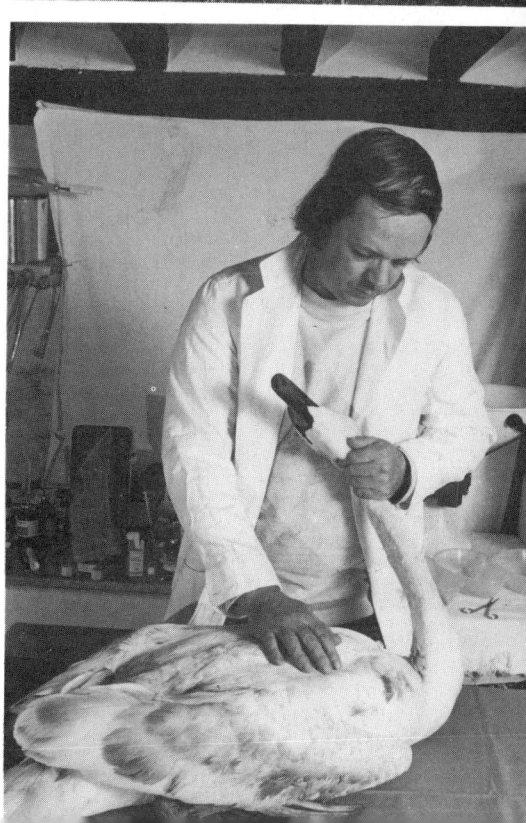

A blanket secures the wings of a swan suffering for the third time from fish-hook and line injuries. Unfortunately, on this occasion some lead had been ingested and this swan was dead within a few days. *(Photo by Paul Scheller)*

Apollo, very ill from lead-poisoning, is still struggling for survival in Len's garden. *(Photo by Paul Felix)*

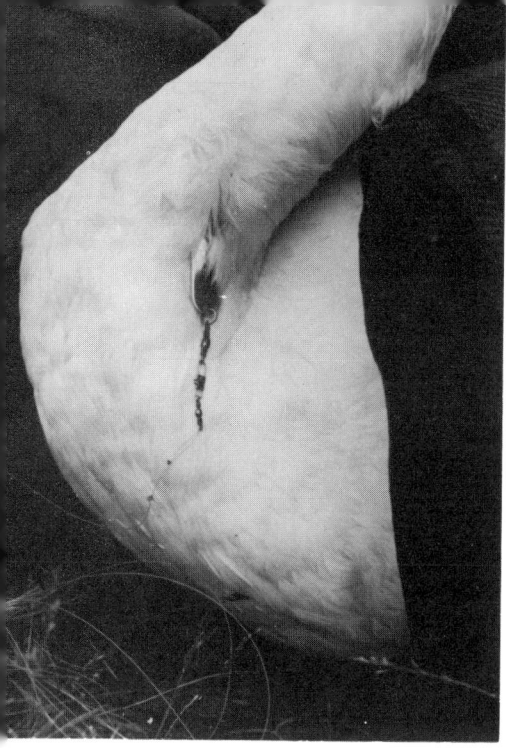

A three-pronged hook especially for pike fishing has embedded itself in this swan's neck. Len was able to remove it by the riverside, stitch the wound and release the bird. *(Photo by Paul Scheller)*

Power cables are the second-biggest cause of death for swans. Lead poisoning ranks first. *(Photo by Paul Scheller)*

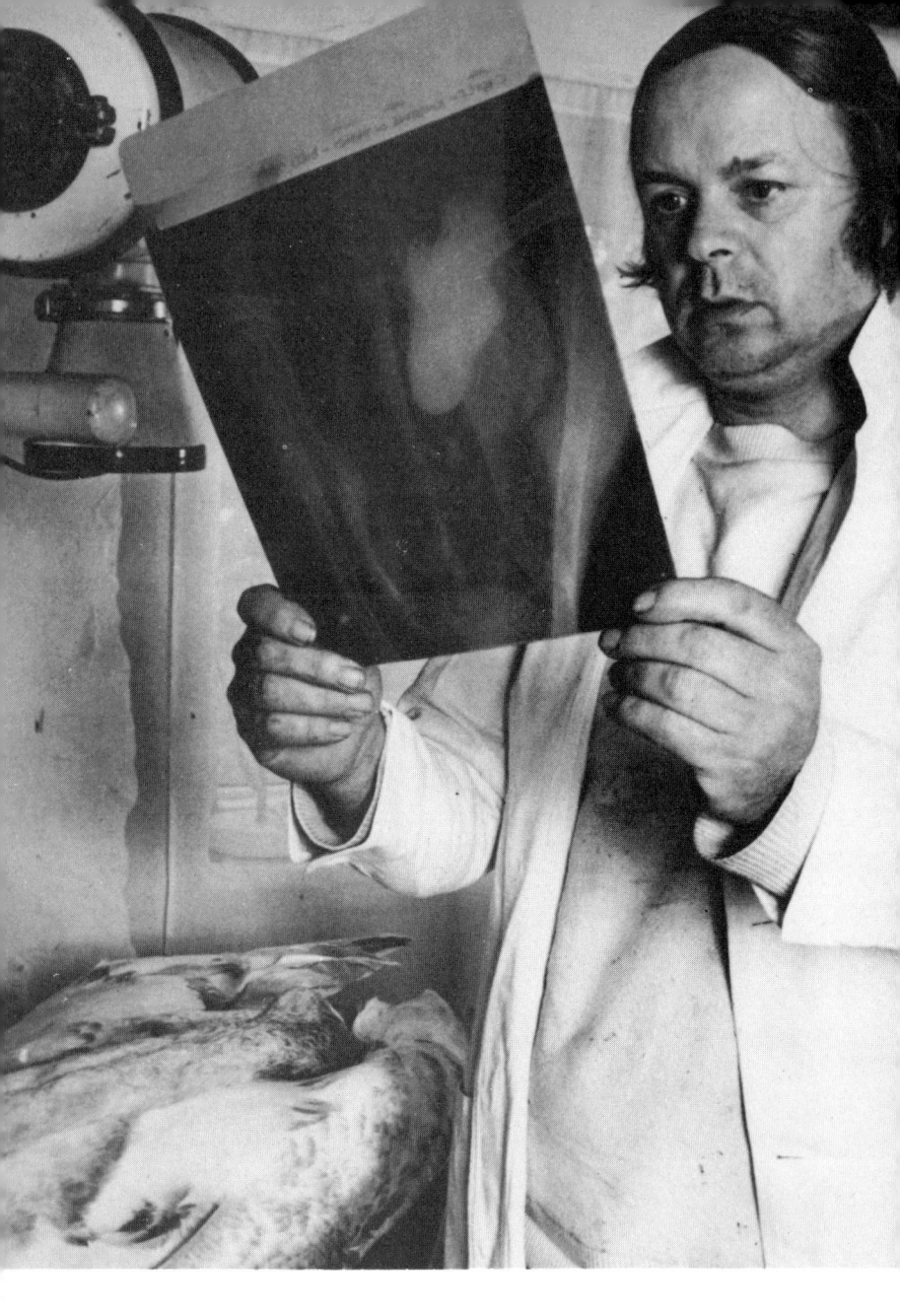

X-rays are a major expense. Often Len has to do up to seventy a week. Here he is looking for lead in the gizzard. *(Photo by Paul Felix)*

Release days are bitter-sweet moments. Here Len and Sheila, helped by Ron and Rose Collins, send some dear friends back to freedom. *(Photo by Lynda Freebrey)*

Lead victim Mr Sunday, now fully recovered and raring to get back to the skies. *(Photo by Jan Tyas, Keystone Press Agency Ltd)*

Len and Sheila with some of their many friends.
(Photo by Syndication International)

which is used to grind down their food. This is stored in the gizzard, a strong, muscular sac which always contains about an eggcupful of grit. The food is ground down to a thick pulp, passed into the intestine, and the nutrients are then dispersed around the swan's body. But when lead is present in the gizzard this simple process is destroyed, for the gizzard is so strong that it is able to grind down the lead too. The toxicity then passes into the bird's bloodstream and reaches all the vital organs, particularly the liver, kidney and brain, and also the bones. But this is not all: in addition the lead attacks the nerve-endings that are present in the walls of the gizzard and gradually paralyses the strong muscles. The gizzard can no longer grind and stays motionless, the food collecting in a hard mass unable to pass through the swan and supply the nutrients needed for survival.

The swan is unaware of what is happening and still feels hungry, so it keeps on eating. It eats and eats until its body, from the gizzard right up the long neck to the throat, becomes impacted with vegetation. The swan is starving to death from lack of nutrition yet its body is solid with food. In this condition, if the swan drinks it may drown because the water is unable to go down the throat and will go into the windpipe, or it will trickle out of the beak leaving the swan still thirsty.

Len believes that it is the impaction of food that is the cause of the kinky neck in lead-poisoned swans, although not all scientists agree with him. They say that the kinky neck is caused by destruction of the neck's nerves and muscles by the lead. Len thinks that is not always so; he maintains that the neck is simply so heavy with the impacted food that the swan literally cannot hold up its head and neck, although there usually is damage to nerves and muscles as well.

At the same time as the collapse of the neck the swan also feels ill. Its vision is impaired, and it is losing co-ordination. Len knows this to be true because he has done some simple tests with his lead-poisoned swans. He has lined up traffic cones in his garden and observed that while healthy swans can pass through the gaps and round the cones, the lead victims walk straight into them. It was obvious that some of the sick swans had no idea the cones were there. Len's power cable fatality figures may verify this fact. Of 49 swans that flew into cables in one year, post-mortems revealed that 37 of them had lead in their gizzards. Len reckons that is too much of a coincidence; his conclusion is that they couldn't see what they were flying into, and even if they had, their co-ordination and reflexes were so damaged that they would have taken evasive action too late.

The standard veterinary treatment for a lead-poisioned swan is to inject it with a drug to fight the toxicity of the lead. This sounds a good idea, and for a long while it was the treatment Len used. But gradually he came to consider that it was, as he now says, 'a load of rubbish'. What is the use, he asks, of pumping a swan full of drugs when the lead that is causing the problem is still in the gizzard? He also became suspicious of the side-effects of drugs. Out of a batch of 35 of his swans injected with the anti-lead drug 33 of them died of something else within six months. Len can't prove this theory, but it has been one of the many things he has worried about. The only answer, he decided, was to get the lead out of the swan.

The answer was presumably surgery. Unfortunately surgery on birds is very difficult: their lungs do not like being under anaesthetic and the recovery rate is not encouraging. And most vets, too, would be hesitant about cutting into a swan's gizzard. So for the time being Len's massaging principle was the right one, although it could not be relied upon to work and he often had to fall back on drugs. The problem, he knew, needed a lot of thought, but ideas were slowly coming to him.

The other human infliction swans suffer is the destruction of their natural and favourite food, reeds. Believing that the swans know what is best for them, and remembering too what the Indian chief had said about a bird showing you how to mend it, Len began looking into reeds. His idea was that perhaps they contain something that could help a swan to fight the lead from the inside; and he had some success.

I was with Len one autumn afternoon when we picked up a sick swan from Oulton Broad. We named him Mr Sunday and he was to be an important landmark in Len's treatment of swans. An X-ray showed that Mr Sunday had seven pieces of anglers' lead in his gizzard, so Len for the first time put his new theory into practice.

This little two-year-old swan was force-fed grit and coarse natural vegetation.

We filled him full of it. For three days and nights we force-fed him in the hope that it would push the lead through the system. We massaged him regularly; he didn't like that, he bit me on the back of my neck and drew blood, but I consoled him and he was okay then.

On the fourth day he definitely looked better and we took him for another X-ray and a miracle had happened, the lead had gone. The vet couldn't believe it either. He asked us how we'd done it. We told him we did nothing, the swan did it.

Len readily admits he was lucky with Mr Sunday, as the lead was in a place where it could be fairly easily dislodged. He did not think for one minute that he had found the absolute answer, although he has used that system successfully many times since. The obvious question still remained: how could he get the lead out of the gizzard with a definite guarantee of success? This problem was to fill his mind for many months.

Len met a particularly beautiful and unusual swan early in 1982, but as usual it was in tragic circumstances. Whoopey stayed with Len and Sheila for thirty-six magical hours. He was a whooper swan, slightly smaller than our mute swans, and he had flown to Britain from Iceland to avoid the terribly cold winter there. He had severe lead-poisoning and X-rays later revealed that he had 74 pieces of gun shot in his gizzard. 'He was a beautiful swan. He'd probably had little contact with humans – whoopers are much wilder than our mutes – but he sat in our kitchen as if he owned the place. He was pure magic. He was the whitest, cleanest swan I've ever seen but he was very sick, and we knew we couldn't save him. He was full of lead.'

Len believes Whoopey had picked up the lead in Scotland as he had made his way down Britain to the warmer south. His entire neck was impacted with the vegetation that he had eaten on the journey. He couldn't eat any more; he just wanted to die. Len and Sheila sat with him for one and a half days. 'He died comfortably, that was all we could do for him,' Len recalls.

Whoopey had a swan trick that Len had never come across before. As they sat nursing him he suddenly lifted his head slightly and cried 'Whoop, whoop!' Within seconds of his call somebody knocked on the Bakers' front door. A few hours later the same thing happened again. Len and Sheila had heard no noises; they hadn't heard the gate open, or footsteps on the path. But little Whoopey had. So Len gave him a test. He left the house, went round the garden, waited for a few minutes and then approached the front door. And before his hand was on the knocker Whoopey had raised his head and given his alarm. He was, it turned out, an ideal watchdog, although his knowledge of residential human life must have been practically nil.

After Whoopey's death Len removed all the vegetation that was in this little swan's throat; it filled a large coffee jar. He keeps it to this day with his many other samples.

Whoopey was found to weigh only 12½lb, much below the weight he should have been. This is another of the results of lead-poisoning: the swans slowly starve to death.

An adult female mute swan should weigh about 24 lb; Alan Hunt has recorded them as low as 10 lb. An adult male should weigh 24-32 lb, but lead has been known to reduce them to 14 lb. The worst case Len has known was a male which died weighing 6 lb. 'He was just bones and feathers. I don't know how he lived as long as he did.'

Scientists and veterinary experts now study lead-poisoning in swans, but few, if any, actually work with them at the level Len does. By doing post-mortems on all his birds, by collecting data, and by just sitting and watching them and their habits, Len claims to be doing the most useful research in the country. (Modesty is not one of his faults!) This is, however, probably true. Other people with whom I have spoken, far better qualified academically than Len, agree that his work is unique, and that he is as much abreast of the problems of lead in swans as anyone in Britain. He has made himself a force to be recognized, and certainly he can no longer be ignored.

Len claims that by living with swans he has got to know the very earliest signs of lead-poisoning. And obviously the earlier it is diagnosed, the sooner the bird can be given treatment and the greater the chances of a successful recovery.

Marlon had been showing symptoms of lead-poisoning just before his death, but in those days Len was not so knowledgeable. The swan had been leaving the water and sitting on the concrete; he had frightened the boatyard cleaning ladies by seeming to be a little aggressive; he had created havoc in the vet's surgery; he had settled on the river away from his nesting site, obviously seeking solitude. These things are all early signs of lead. But there are others. A swan with lead will start to bump into things, he will trip up, and to the trained eye he will appear lethargic. He will keep shaking his head and sometimes gasp for breath. 'It's taken a long while to get to know all these things, but now I can look at a flock of swans and pick out those with lead long before their necks start going kinky. I bet there are few scientists, or vets, who can do that.'

Which raises another sore point with Len. He says there are too many scientists using swans as guinea-pigs to 'discover' repeatedly what is already known – namely, that swans die from lead-poisoning. Not enough scientists or vets are trying actually to cure the swans, he says. He accuses the experts of not caring.

They examine tha birds, discover they've got lead-poisoning and put them back into the water. When the swan is dead they cut up the body and confirm again that it had lead. They've got lots of records proving that lots of swans get lead-poisoning, but hardly anyone is trying to save the swans' lives.

Other Threats from Angling

Fly swan. Go somewhere else,
Somewhere where pain is unknown.
I wish I could come with you.
Still – perhaps I can.

Lead-poisoning is undoubtedly the largest single threat to swans. But the danger from anglers does not end there, for swans also suffer and die from injuries caused by the fisherman's hooks and line.

Since Len began his work with swans he estimates that the average number of deaths he has seen that were caused by fishing is about 90 per cent. Last year, 1982, the fatality rate due to fishing was 92 per cent. In April of that year Len sent a batch of 62 swans back to freedom, having cured them and nursed them lovingly. Within six months 58 of these swans were dead. All but one had died from angling accidents or lead-poisoning; the one that escaped the fishermen was caught by a power cable. His cygnet mortality rate in 1982 was 85 per cent, and the majority of those deaths were caused by angling, either accidents or lead.

These statistics are no doubt upsetting to the dedicated, caring angler who, with his experience and professional approach to the sport, has never hurt a swan in his life; but unfortunately the dedicated, caring anglers are in the minority.

It is estimated that six people every hour of every day take up fishing. The majority of those will be given no guidance, no teaching, and probably will not even read a book on the subject.

They will buy, or be given, a rod and will simply go fishing, totally unaware of the dangers they can inflict upon the river birds.

Angling is the largest participant outdoor sport in Britain. At the height of the fishing season there are more people on the banks of our rivers, canals and lakes than there are at football matches all over the country. It is estimated that 8 per cent of the total population fish; and that 50 per cent of all men and boys over the age of twelve take to the sport. There are over 3,250,000 anglers, over 2,250,000 of whom have taken up coarse fishing, that is fishing on rivers. The remainder are either game or sea anglers, who do not present the same threat to swans as river fishermen.

Of these three million anglers only one-third belong to clubs. Even if all club members behave perfectly, are given good instruction, never drop one lead weight and always take their tackle home with them, there are still enough thoughtless amateurs to go on killing swans. There are children who accidentally hook a swan, panic, throw their rod into the water, run home and say nothing. That night a swan is dying in the reeds in dreadful pain with a hook, line and rod dragging it down. There are anglers who, perhaps by mistake, hook a swan and not knowing what to do cut the line to allow the swan to swim away. They have not really helped the swan, which of course is unable to disentangle itself from the line. But the biggest danger of all, and one that is repeated daily up and down the lengths of our waterways, is the careless angler who discards his line and tackle at the end of his day's fishing. Such people do not even bother to find a litter bin, or better still take their rubbish home to their own dustbin, but just throw it on to the ground or into the river. These are the people Len calls murderers.

Fishing tackle these days is comparatively cheap. Before the last war anglers used silk line, which was expensive, and also tougher. It could be rewound for another day's use, and because of its price that is exactly what most anglers would do. But since the fifties the introduction of nylon line has changed the anglers' attitudes. It is relatively cheap and many of them therefore throw away what they no longer want. And because it breaks far more easily than the old silk line, more is discarded. Weights are not a big expense to today's fisherman either, as was proved by the 3,000 pieces of fishing lead found on riverbanks by youngsters on a project

71

already described.

The fishing tackle made these days is also very cruel. Fine nylon line can cut through a swan's beak like cheese-wire, says Len. It can entangle the body, pin down wings, entwine necks and limbs and cut into the flesh. When swallowed it is amassed into choking lumps, or sits in the swan's gizzard instead of rotting away as silk line would have done. The gizzard cannot crush it so it forms into a kind of hard scouring pad, blocking the normal flow of food and eventually starving the bird to death. Len once dealt with a swan whose tongue had been tied to its bottom bill by line that had become wound round and round it. That swan would have starved to death too.

When discarded on banks the nylon line will lie there indefinitely, posing all these potential hazards for the swans.

Fish-hooks too are lethal objects. Many are barbed, making the pain worse for the swan when one becomes embedded in its flesh or mouth or throat, and of course making the job of removal much more difficult.

And alongside all this we have also had a considerable expansion in the number of anglers. Since the fifties the numbers have steadily increased, the current estimated figure of 3,380,000 has never been higher.

Karla and Karl II had six cygnets in June 1982, but within seven weeks two of them were dead and one was seriously injured. Len was called by a fisherman to see to one of them. The angler had noticed the cygnet in the reeds all by itself and thought that something must be wrong. He met Len on the riverbank and was astounded to be told that the cygnet's kinky neck indicated lead-poisoning. The fisherman, a stranger to Len, wanted to know more. What was lead-poisoning? How did swans get it? Would the cygnet die? As Len answered the man's questions he could see that the angler was becoming both enraged and ashamed. He could not believe that he and his sport were such a threat to the swans. He was genuinely ignorant of the facts. 'But in anger he kicked his bait box and knocked a load of lead weights all over the place. We both spent ages on our hands and knees picking it all up. He frightened me a bit; he was absolutely enraged, and told me he would never fish again in his life.'

The cygnet, just under seven weeks old, died two days later in Len's arms. An X-ray showed no lead in his gizzard which meant that he had ground it all down, resulting in a massive overdose to his tiny system. He had never flown, and had hardly even got used to swimming. During his seven short weeks on this earth he had known sickness, pain, paralysis and bewilderment. As Len asks himself time and time again, what on earth have swans ever done to deserve all this?

Karla's second cygnet died the same week, again from lead. An X-ray showed a 2 ounce lead ledger weight in the gizzard. These weights are ironically known as coffin weights because of their shape; this one measured just over an inch long and half an inch thick. The cygnet died within hours of Len being called. 'He died in our kitchen. He was miserable and sick. He just tucked his little beak under his wing and died.'

Their sister, to be named Karlee, was four weeks old when a holidaymaker telephoned Len to tell him that a cygnet was in trouble. Karlee had a fish hook in her throat and the line was tangled in an overhanging tree. The tide had turned and was pulling her down stream, but of course she was tethered. She had been like that for about three hours when Len cut her free. She had a 1½ inch tear down into her throat where the barbs had become embedded in her flesh as she had tried to swallow the hook; the line Len cut her from measured 40 feet. She was in a bad state of shock. At the time of writing little Karlee was still in the Bakers' courtyard.

'She's not really responding to treatment. She's hardly grown, and her morale is down. She's missing her mum and dad, and her freedom, but I can't let her go yet, she couldn't fend for herself as she is at the moment.'

That year three of Karla's cygnets made it through their first fishing season, which was quite an achievement, for the year before she and Karl II had seven cygnets, all but one of which died. Four of those died from lead-poisoning and two from fish-hooks. The one which survived had a fish-hook in his beak but Len was able to tend to him on the riverbank. He ringed him and sent him off to freedom. The swan disappeared from the area and Len has never seen him again, which is unusual, for Len is usually able to follow the fortunes of all his swans and their families. If

73

you meet a swan on your travels, see if he has a white plastic ring on his leg with the number 077 in black letters. If so perhaps you would let Len know, for he is Marlon's grandson and Len is worried about him.

Swan 031 probably had the worst death that Len has ever witnessed. A swan could hardly have suffered more. There is a pub in Norwich called Gibraltar Gardens that is popular with anglers, and 031 unfortunately lived nearby. One of the Swan Rescue team found him with fishing line and a hook in his throat.

We brought him home and treated him, but he still didn't look well, we couldn't understand it. He was very weak and he had the mark of death on him. We made him as comfortable as we could but over a period of two days he deteriorated even more. I was beginning to think I would have to have him put down when he beat us to it; he quietly died. At the post-mortem it was found that his entire gizzard and his throat were completely full of the most disgusting, rotten vegetation. The normal diameter of a swan's throat is about one inch. This swan's throat had been stretched to nearly two inches, and his gizzard, instead of being the normal two inches in diameter, was extended to six inches. Full of impacted muck, hay, bread and gunge. His gizzard was paralysed. What we removed from him filled a litre size ice cream carton.

He was in a terrible mess, but worse was to come. As if he hadn't suffered enough we then found an airgun pellet embedded in the base of his neck. That was wicked; 031 was the worst mess I've ever seen. The inside of a swan is usually as beautiful as the outside. The design is incredible, but this little bird was far from beautiful. We discovered that he also had four different types of worms attacking his body. His gizzard, which should be strong, just crumbled as it was touched, it was full of worms. As well as all the pain from the hook, airgun pellet and lead poisoning he was slowly being eaten away. The worms had attacked him because he was so run down, but it was the lead that had done that to him and it was the lead that finally killed him.

It was Christmas morning and Len and Sheila's present to each other was going to be a well deserved lie-in, surely not over-indulgent on this special day. But the inevitable happened: at 7.25 a.m. on this freezing cold morning the telephone rang. A lady at nearby Stoke Holy Cross had not wanted to trouble them on Christmas Day, she was very apologetic, but she had been out walking her dog and had seen a swan with an unusual lump, or growth, under its beak. By 7.50 Len and Sheila were on the scene. They had not even had a cup of tea, but had just thrown on some clothes and headed for the location given. They began their search along the riverbank, but two hours later they had found nothing.

We really searched every inch of riverbank and could find nothing. It was bitter. There was no one around, just a few birds; apart from that the whole world seemed still. Just us, shivering and frozen to the core looking for a swan. We decided to have one more good search then we'd have to call it a day and go home for something hot to drink.

Len and Sheila separated. She walked the three-quarters of a mile up the inside bend of the river while Len did the mile on the outside of the bend.

We couldn't feel our feet and fingers, they were numb from coldness. Our lips were practically freezing together, and we could hardly talk properly to each other. It was crazy, so we decided to give up, go home, get warm and come out again later in the day.

As they crossed a tiny footbridge on their way back to the car the sky was black and very threatening. Then out of the blackness came two white shapes.

We thought they were gulls, and we gazed at them thinking how striking they looked against the dark sky. But as they flew nearer we realized they were swans. They flew round and round in circles above our heads. Now swans are shrewd, they've come to know that humans mean bread, and we assumed they had spotted us and come for a Christmas Day snack with us. They got lower and lower, skimming over the

75

few isolated buildings dotted around. I knew they wouldn't land by us; swans can land on the ground but they prefer water, which meant these swans had got to go behind us and back towards the river that we had just left. But they didn't. They wouldn't leave us – they flew so close to our heads that the breeze from their wings fluttered our hair. When they were sure they had got our attention they went towards the river and landed together. Something told us something was going on. The whole event seemed uncanny. We felt they were beckoning us to follow, so we did follow, and we found that they had landed one each side of the injured swan that we hadn't been able to find.

The sickly swan was retrieved from the river while the other two looked on. A fishhook had embedded itself in the swan's throat, but it was an easy job to remove it and by 11.45 the swan was back in the river with his friends. The lump had been caused by vegetation that had become caught up around the hook. Soon the Bakers were speeding home for a hot cup of coffee and a cheese sandwich. They did three more rescues on that particular Christmas Day.

Sheila and I are convinced those two swans led us to their injured friend. They had seen us searching, they had been watching us from the sky although we hadn't noticed them. When they realized we were turning away from the river and going away they swooped down and led us back. That was the most wonderful Christmas present of our entire lives.

Many people will laugh at a man's claim to have such a rapport with a wild bird, but Len is convinced he has. He doesn't understand why, but events such as this have happened to him and Sheila many times – too often, he says, for them to be coincidences. Not that he takes it for granted. Relationships with swans, just as with humans, have to be worked at. Theirs is a very special love affair, with the two parties not always understanding the other's ways, but after six years Len has probably got closer to swans than anyone else in the country.

A beautiful swan called Zorba began his relationship with Len on quite the wrong foot. He too fell victim to the angler when he got a fish-hook in his head.

Getting to him was easy, for he was right by the bank and he let me pull him out of the water with no objections at all. The hook was easy to remove; it didn't even bleed. It just took a couple of minutes and he was as good as new again. He seemed reluctant to go back into the water so I gave his tail feathers a gentle tap and said, 'Go on old chap, you're okay now,' and suddenly I felt a blow across my face. He had spun round like a spinning-top and bashed me with his right wing. I fell to my knees, blood pouring from my mouth. He'd knocked out four of my teeth and broken a fifth one in half. I was definitely off him! The pain was beyond belief.

As it happens Zorba and his lady Zoretta were to become very close to Len and Sheila, later allowing them a specially magical moment with one of their cygnets. But as Len struggled on the riverbank, with no handkerchief but just a piece of screwed up paper to mop up the blood, his feelings for Zorba were far from magical. And to make matters worse he suddenly heard a very upper-crust voice asking: 'I say, do you think you could face the camera?'

Mackerel hooks, as their name suggests, are used by anglers to catch mackerel, and they are bigger and cause more injury than ordinary fish-hooks. Little Stracey Gem, as he was to become called, had four of them in his body when Len was called to his rescue. They had been in him for some time, so that he had become unable to walk and was swimming lopsided in the water. Len found him sitting on his own in one of the most heavily fished areas of the Broads. He borrowed a dinghy from a helpful holidaymaker and rowed over to him. Stracey Gem put up no resistance and allowed himself to be lifted from the water and into the boat. When Len got him home he couldn't believe what he saw. 'There was one mackerel hook in his foot with a nine-inch piece of line going to another hook in his wing bone. There was a third hook in the top of his leg and when I did another thorough check over his little body I found a fourth hook, practically hidden underneath the wing.'

Because of the line running between the hooks the swan had become like a puppet. When he moved one part of himself other parts moved too. If he lifted his wing he yanked his foot out of the water; if he tried to use his foot he pulled his wing down. Life was ridiculing this elegant bird, who was suffering the pain and indignity as nobly as he could. 'We got the lot off him. We worked on him through the night, using our absolute magic potion, Friars Balsam, straight on to the wounds; it makes the blood congeal immediately, we'd be lost without the stuff. It took a few hours, but we got Stracey Gem as well as we could.'

This swan was in a very bad way. Apart from his injuries his immobility had meant that he could not search for food and he had been slowly starving. Every day for a month he was massaged. Sheila rubbed Johnson's baby oil into his injured foot every morning and eventually he walked, although he limped for a long while. After two months he was released, well and happy.

> I've put him on a private stretch of river that is fenced at both ends. He lives in peace there with a ladyfriend he has met. I've given him to a landowner, who from his family records says there had been swans on his land for five hundred years but he had lost them all, many he knows died from lead-poisoning. He's banned fishing on his land now, so Stracey Gem will be safe.

Perverted people come in all shapes and sizes, and the angling fraternity has its quota. Len has known of people deliberately casting at swans. He has known of swans having their eyes pierced by hooks. He remembers one particular cygnet, just ten days old, that was taunted by two men on a holiday cruiser. Eye-witnesses told Len that the men, fishing from the boat, had deliberately hooked the little bird and had played with it for over twenty minutes. The hook was through the left leg and they kept yanking the cygnet towards them, allowing it to swim away, and then yanking it back again. They broke the leg and then laughed as they cut the line and left the area, leaving the cygnet with the hook and line still attached to its broken limb.

Len's growing reputation as one who broadcasts the threat

posed by anglers to the river birds has made him unpopular among many fishermen. A local angler, fed up with what he regarded as Len's interference, was seen to tip a tobacco tin full of lead shot into the river, saying as he did it, 'That's for Swan Rescue.'

Life from a swan's-eye view is not a happy one. Due to circumstances beyond their control, cygnets are born into the world at the peak of the holiday season and the start of the fishing season. They quickly learn, because their parents show them, that if they go up to a boat the humans will give them bread. So they get used to obtaining food in that way. But come October all the boats go, the holidaymakers disappear, and the swans find that their food supply has vanished. The reeds that should form the basis of their diet have been eroded and killed by heavy boating. The next best thing is grass or grain, so the swans climb out of the rivers and walk on the land, where they often get shot by farmers.

During all this time they are dodging the hazards that surround them from anglers and from boats. If they survive the summer and actually make it to being a fully-fledged bird at about four and a half months of age, they probably look around and think that since there is no food, they might as well fly somewhere else to look for some. If they do take off they stand a high chance of hitting a power cable and being electrocuted. 'How the hell can these birds win? They've got no chance of surviving in this world. They are doomed, and nobody seems to care.'

In his darkest moments Len really does feel that he is fighting a losing battle. It breaks his heart when swans that he has rescued, treated and cured appear back in his courtyard with new injuries. Some swans seem to suffer so much, so many times. When old friends like Marlon die, and there have been many such dear friends, a little of Len dies too. He is not ashamed to say that he sheds a tear when these beautiful creatures quietly lay their heads on his knee as if asking him to help them, and he knows nothing more can be done for them. He admits too that he has become ashamed of mankind. Without man swans would have none of the pain inflicted by power cables, roads, trains, boats and lead. But he knows that it would be unfair to paint us all with the same brush, for many people show that they do care, they care very much.

79

Two local policemen are on Len's list of caring humans, and he remembers them with much affection. Len had been called to a swan that was bleeding badly from the throat. Unable to get to the swan, he enlisted the help of the two policemen, Bob and Gordon. The swan had a fish-hook in its throat and was shaking its head furiously. Len and his two helpers pursued the swan until it became trapped in a dyke, but the swan, realizing this, climbed out of the water and into a marshy, reed area nearby. Neither Len nor the policemen had waterproof clothing with them, not even wellingtons, and they all ended up soaked to the skin.

We had to follow the swan. He needed help quickly, but he was panicking. The reeds were at least eight feet tall, so we three couldn't even see each other, let alone a tiny swan. It was like looking for a needle in a sopping wet haystack.

It was very quiet. I was standing absolutely still trying to hear the swan moving, and I could hear soft breathing.

Slowly I moved towards the spot, trying not to make a noise, and I was just about to leap when this policeman's beaming face peered at me through the reeds. We were about to leap on each other! We were laughing at the ridiculous situation when a gentle hiss came towards us through the reeds.

The swan was caught and Len took him home. In honour of his rescuers he was named Constable and he lived with the Bakers for five weeks while his wound healed. He was a very friendly swan, and he provided Len and Sheila with one of their uncanny experiences.

They released Constable at a place called Stokesby, but he flew away, where to the Bakers had no idea. A few weeks later they were called to a small village a few miles from Stokesby to remove a hook from a swan. It was an easy job and they were just about to return to their car when suddenly they saw an unusual sight: a flock of swans, well over thirty of them, came swimming under the bridge. The Bakers had to stop and admire them.

It looked like a big white cloud floating down the river; it was magnificent. And Sheila pointed excitedly at one of them and said, 'Look, there's Constable,' Now, I felt there was no way

Marlon — the swan that will stay for ever in Len's heart.

Len and Sheila. *(Photo by Syndication International)*

Above: Pawline, Marlon's lady, was killed by a crossbow bolt, but not before sharing many swan secrets with Len.

Left: Pawline's only surviving cygnet, Karl, with Karla. They were to nest just seven yards from Pawline and Marlon.

Below: Swans love car travel and, with the aid of the car's two-way radio — a gift from an anonymous well-wisher — Len is able to speed from emergency to emergency. *(Photo by Paul Felix)*

Swan suffering

Above: Three-year-old Ticky's broken neck was caused by beating with a stick.

Left: Hooks in beaks are commonplace. This lucky swan was treated successfully by the riverside and swam to freedom. *(Photo by Paul Scheller)*

Below: Broken wings are often the result of hitting power cables. This swan recovered from its chest burns but had to have its wing amputated.

One day's recovery of dead swans from local rivers.

Little Haddiscoe, the brave victim of a wing amputation — after hitting a cable, falling to the ground, being hit by a car and then being harassed by bullocks.

Buxton, convalescing after losing an eye to an airgun pellet.
He will be staying with Len until he's adapted to seeing with one eye.
(Photo by Paul Felix)

Lady Wednesday — the first of Swan Rescue's long-term patients.

Lake Marlon, the hand-dug lake in Len's swan sanctuary, now the home for scores of convalescing and visiting birds. *(Photo by Paul Felix)*

À la carte treatment for Tom and his lady from the staff of the Hilton Hotel, Stratford.

that Sheila could recognize a swan out of over thirty, and from such a distance. I tried to change the subject, for I knew it would upset her if she was wrong. I took her hand and tried to make her climb up the bank to the car, but she insisted. 'That's Constable,' she said, 'the third one from the left.'

Sheila was adamant and she shouted out Constable's name as loud as she could. Len could hardly believe what happened next. The swan separated himself from the flock and crossed the river. He swam straight up to Sheila and stood up in the water with his wings out. It was definitely Constable, for the scar on his throat was there as proof. He hissed gently at Sheila as if to say hello, and then swam back towards his new friends.

Swan Populations

There is no finality.
Perfection and beauty
Cannot simply cease to be.

No one knows exactly how many swans there are in Britain. Some experts maintain that the population has declined, while others argue that sensible swans have simply moved to quieter spots away from humanity and that their numbers remain more or less the same.

Not many people, however, would argue that there has been a drastic decline in the number of swans on many of our rivers. And even if the redistribution theory proves to be true, the fact remains that many river swans of Britain have either been killed or frightened away.

In bygone days swans were under attack for different reasons. Their quills were used for pens, their down for bedding. Four-teenth-century records refer to shipwrecked men floating on rafts made from swans down. On the command to abandon ship they would tie knots in the corners of their swansdown beds (similar to today's duvets), throw themselves overboard and hang on to the knotted corners for grim death as their floatable bed tossed on the waves.

Quills were used for various purposes: the thicker ones as bottle stoppers, safety valves, and when fermenting yeast and ale, and smaller ones as teats for feeding young lambs and even babies. The wing ends were used as small brushes, the larger feathers tied together and used for sweeping up corn.

While swans for food and swansdown always fetched a good price, the other parts of the swan's anatomy were commonly available and do not appear to have had any scarcity value.

It was not until 1955 that the first national census of swans was conducted in this country. Organized by the British Trust for Ornithology, it revealed that in England and Wales there were 14,300-15,300 birds, including 3,000-3,500 breeding pairs; in Scotland, 3,500-4,000 birds, including 463 breeding pairs: a total of between 17,800 and 19,300 birds.

The census showed that the highest numbers of swans were to be found in south-east England, the Thames Valley, the Midlands, Norfolk and Somerset – precisely the areas, perhaps with the exception of Somerset, where swans have come under the greatest threat and where their numbers are known to have declined.

A further survey, conducted by Malcolm Ogilvie of the Wildfowl Trust in 1978, showed a decline on the 1955 figures of between 8 and 15 per cent, and perhaps more significantly it showed a drop in the numbers of breeding pairs, while non-breeding adults were more plentiful.

One does not need to be a scientist or an ornithologist to be able to see that areas in which swans once flourished have now lost these beautiful birds, and possibly lost them for ever.

The Thames is a good example. In 1955/6 the annual swan-upping figures revealed that there were, 1,100 swans: by 1972 this had declined to 399. In 1981 the figure had fallen to 153, and by 1982 was a mere 112 adults and 84 cygnets.

As the Nature Conservancy Council report says, the large urban flocks which were characteristic of the Thames have now completely gone.

At Stratford-upon-Avon the picture is equally distressing. Joe Hardman, an agricultural scientist who lives near Stratford, has for some twenty years studied, and generally watched over, the local swans. Although he is no more than a keen amateur enthusiast, Joe Hardman's work and the results he has published have gained respect within expert circles, and indeed were used as a point of reference by the NCC working group on swans.

Joe estimates that about twenty years ago there were 60-70 swans at Stratford. The 1955 census had revealed 40, but by 1959, a year generally accepted as being peak year for swan populations nationally, the numbers at Stratford had risen to around 100 and the local Council was expressing concern at what seemed to be a continuing expansion of the swan flock. There was even a suggestion that culling might be necessary to reduce numbers by 50 per cent. However, a decline set in without such direct interference.

In 1961 the numbers were down to 62, and they have since dwindled annually until today there are just two swans left.

There was one major acceleration in the decline of the Stratford swans in 1974 and 1975, and post-mortems revealed the killer to have been the ingestion of fishing weights followed by the inevitable lead-poisoning. These were known as the 'lead kill' years, although Joe Hardman emphasizes that lead is not alone in the destruction of the swan flock. Over the years there has also been an increase in boating in the area, with inevitable destruction of the weeds and vegetation needed by the swans. Swans are also known to have flown away to new areas.

Since 1962, Joe Hardman's studies have revealed that on the Warwickshire Avon as a whole there has been a severe decline in the total swan populations, involving a reduction of non-breeders by more than half, and the complete loss of the Stratford flock. Breeding pairs on the Avon have dropped by one-third, and their breeding success by a quarter. He maintains that lead-poisoning caused by ingestion of fishing weights was responsible for three-quarters of the swan deaths, the remainder having died because they could not cope with the deterioration of their habitat caused by boating, dredging and the consequent lack of food.

Stratford's two remaining swans are local celebrities. The male, affectionately known as Tom, is thought to be about five years old. He has had a hard life. His first mate, Sue, had eight eggs in 1981 but they were all washed away by a freak rainstorm. The same season Sue had four more eggs. These hatched successfully, but all the cygnets were lost within a few weeks: two died from lead-poisoning, one was involved in a fishing-line accident and drowned, the death of the fourth remained a mystery. Then early in 1982 Sue died from lead-poisoning. Now Tom has a new ladyfriend. She was too young at first to have cygnets, but everyone is hoping that she will soon be introduced to mother-hood.

Joe Hardman's findings made it abundantly clear that Tom and his mate, and any future swans, needed help from man in order to survive. So a group of local swan-lovers, including Joe and the Mayor, got together to raise £10,000 for the establishing of a 'safe' lagoon in which the swans could live, away from the menaces of the river Avon. Stratford's residents, and presumably many visitors to this famous town, rallied to the call and the money was raised within a year.

The lagoon was built on land donated by the Stratford Hilton Hotel. It is one acre of water within a four acre landscaped site. Fishing is not allowed, nor is boating. Joe has advised on the aquatic vegetation to be planted, but this will take some time to establish itself and to flourish in sufficient quantities to feed hungry swans. In the meantime the daily job of feeding Tom and his lady has fallen to the Hilton's Front Office Manager Cyril Bennis. He gives them a bucketful of grain a day, and Tom now recognizes his voice and appears on the scene when Cyril calls. His mate is still a little shy, but follows at a safe distance behind Tom.

The two swans will never know to what lengths the local people have gone in an attempt to save their lives and give them a safe home. But a few corks will be popping to wet the new cygnets' heads, when the time comes. Meanwhile Stratford is keeping its fingers crossed.

Early in 1982 the Royal Society for the Protection of Birds launched a campaign to save the swans in Wales. Numbers had dropped alarmingly, they said, and their campaign was aimed at preventing the swan from becoming extinct in Wales.

Roger Lovegrove of the RSPB Welsh office told me that as recently as ten years ago he estimated that there were over 200 breeding pairs in Wales; now there are only 85.

Last year, 1983, the British Trust for Ornithology and Malcolm Ogilvie of the Wildfowl Trust combined forces to conduct another national survey. Their findings will be published soon, and until then all estimates of swan populations can be no more than intelligent guesses. Malcolm Ogilvie, a research officer with the Wildfowl Trust, has spent much time looking into swan population and he considers that there are probably about 4,000 breeding pairs in England and Wales.

A bird population specialist at the British Trust for Ornithology, David Glue, told me:

The picture in the Midlands, the Broads, and the Thames is causing concern. Nest sites have been disturbed and vegetation eroded. Swans are tolerant birds, very resilient to many things. They can put up with a great deal before they give up, but they can't fight lead. Even flying into overhead cables is something they can learn not to do, especially the mature birds, and even coping with the loss of vegetation isn't beyond them. But lead? No, they can't cope with lead.

Swans cannot colonize old areas again – because the destruction lasts for years – although they will try. They are unlikely ever to return to places from which they have been driven. The River Trent in Nottingham is one such place.

Alan Hunt, clinical biochemist at the MAFF veterinary investigation centre at Sutton Bonnington, remembers Nottingham in the seventies when there were about fifty swans there. They have all died, and they all went to him for post-mortems; over ninety-five per cent of them had lead-poisoning. Says Alan: 'Anglers like the redistribution theory; they say swans sense the danger and leave. The Nottingham swans didn't fly away, they died, and we post-mortemed them.'

Scientists name some areas 'biological sinks'. The Trent, the Avon and the Thames are among those sinks. Alan Hunt again: 'The swans have gone from these areas now, and even if a new bird lands it will be dead within two or three months, from lead.'

Alan has personal memories of other areas. He can recall Leicester in the seventies when it also had some 50 swans. Today there are about nine. At Burton-upon-Trent there used to be over 40; about one dozen still survive.

And at Mistley, in Essex, home of the tipsy swans described earlier, locals claim there used to be hundreds of swans – the figure of 800 is believed by many. Now there are 135, and many of those are ill.

Len Baker maintains that there probably isn't a place in England that has not seen a decline in the number of swans. If you live in a village, town or city with a river or canal in or near it, it might be interesting to do some local research and, if you can, establish how many swans your neighbourhood once had. You are likely to be in for a shock.

Swan Love

I cannot fly as you,
I am not formed of feathers
And freedom.
But my thoughts fly
Even as high as your
Highest winging ways.
Often, when the pain
Catches the voice
And a sentence
Is cut short
I take to your sky . . .
And I am with you.

If man's cruelty has broken Len's heart, it is the swans' love that has healed it. Their love for each other, and for Len and Sheila, is something that perhaps many people will have trouble in accepting. To be honest, I am not sure whether I believe it myself or not, but I know that Len most certainly does, and he is the one who spends every day, and most nights, with the swans. It is a fact that a swan becomes calm when Len walks near; this I have seen. It is true that hissing, aggressive swans are often pacified by him. Swans will, and often do, submit to his presence and allow themselves to be lifted out of the water, put into his car, and driven away. Other people who have been near swans report of vicious attacks, pecking and hissing. Len has had some bad moments with panicking swans, but usually they seem to sense that he has come to help them.

One vet I spoke to, who has seen Len working with swans, commented that it was amazing how they will calmly sit and let

Len do many things to them. Can they sense that this man and his wife are their very special friends?

Zorba, you remember, was the swan who hit Len across the face and knocked out his front teeth. A rude introduction to what was to become a beautiful friendship, which presented one of those mystical moments that Len cannot explain but claims happen often.

One beautiful summer's day in 1981 Len was told that a cygnet on a nearby river was looking bad. He sensed it was Zorba's family that was in trouble and went immediately. Zorba and Zoretta had six cygnets and Len could see that one was looking slow in the water and hanging behind the others. Zoretta kept going back to it, trying to scurry it along and make it keep up with the rest of the family. A rescue would have to be done, Len could see that. Not an easy task, and Len still had his memories!

The next morning Len and Sheila gathered up their courage to tackle the problem. They found the little family on a bank in one of the broads. Len has not got many golden rules when dealing with swans, but a definite one is never to approach a swan family when they are out of the water. Zorba and Co. were out of the water. The sick cygnet by now had blood bubbling out of its nostrils. Time was of the essence and Len couldn't wait until Zorba decided to go back into the water. They borrowed a boat and quietly moved towards the swans. Len readily admits now that he was scared, but he had no choice. And anyway, he thought, you can only lose your teeth once!

But as the boat sidled up to the bank Sheila took the situation into her own hands. Before Len could stop her she was out of the boat and on to the bank.

I called after her to come back, I was frightened for her. I thought Zorba would attack her and if so she wouldn't have stood a chance: she's only little and Zorba was huge. And then something magical happened, I couldn't believe it. I just watched spellbound. Sheila stepped gingerly over the little cygnets and Zorba and Zoretta parted to give her room so that she could reach their sick baby. She picked it up and carefully trod back over them all again and got back into the boat. And not a murmur from Zorba or Zoretta. They silently watched us move away, they put up no fight at all.

They knew Sheila and I were trying to help. Their baby was sick, and they trusted us. I call that love.

The little cygnet died at 11 o'clock that night. A post-mortem the following day showed that it had been killed by a fish-hook ripping into its windpipe. It was four days old.

Did the parent swans sense that Sheila had been sent to help? We will never know. But it is true that they parted to give her room, when normally a swan would fight to stop anyone from taking a cygnet. Remember Marlon and how he attacked Len savagely when his sick cygnet had to be removed? This protection of their young is surely part of the love bond.

The greatest love I've ever witnessed is between swans and their babies. Come March and the time for the cygnets to go, mum and dad kick them out. They reared them, fed them, protected them, showed them how to survive, but now they must go it alone. For above everything a swan is independent. The father returns to protecting his own territory and even his own offspring aren't allowed in his stretch of water. If one of those cygnets returns the father will kill it, because it means the swan is weak and it won't survive. And if while they're still living with the parents a cygnet becomes ill, again, the father will kill it. He'll hold the baby under the water until the bubbles stop coming up. It takes about eight seconds, then he lets the body float away. Perhaps it sounds cruel, but it's not, it's a great love. A weak cygnet will not survive, it will suffer pain, injury, perhaps be eaten alive by rats, perhaps die very, very slowly. This way is quick; it is fatherly love.

That swans mate for life is also often true, although the death toll on many of our rivers means that there are many 'widows' and 'widowers' who very often find new partners. And, says Len, you do sometimes get the odd separation, although couples usually stay together.

Marlon, however, had the best of both worlds. When he and Pawline were nesting under their 7 knots speed limit sign Len and Sheila noticed that every Sunday Marlon would disappear for a while. Not on any other day of the week, just on Sundays. Why Sundays? What was special about Sundays? It puzzled them so they schemed a plot and decided to follow him. At the crack of dawn the next Sunday Len and Sheila were hiding in the reeds in a small dinghy. All was well with the world. Pawline was on the nest sleeping contentedly; Marlon was attempting to look nonchalant. Then, at ten minutes past six, Marlon took off. Very quietly he slipped into the water and without waking Pawline he turned right, paddled downstream as silently as was possible for a swan, and was away. Pawline slept on, unaware that her mate and protector had slunk off. Using just one paddle Len and Sheila followed quietly in the dinghy, staying well back but keeping their eyes on this adventurer.

Half a mile later Marlon came to a junction; to his left was a little stream. He looked around furtively, as if checking to see whether Pawline was following. No, she wasn't, so he swam into the stream. Len and Sheila followed.

And there, a little way up the stream, lived a most beautiful lady swan. She was lovely. And Marlon obviously thought so too. He swam up to her, and she wasn't a bit surprised, she'd obviously been expecting him. They bathed together and had a necking session; nothing too serious, then they said goodbye and Marlon swam all the way home again. He got back to Pawline, who was awake by now, and told her he'd just been checking out their territory and that there were no enemies around.

The little swan probably never knew that the admirer who came courting every Sunday was a married man and an expectant father to boot! And Len and Sheila never let on to Pawline for after all, even among swans, ignorance is bliss.

Swans do, somehow, in their own quiet, serene way, seem to stimulate love. While people will say they love cats but not dogs, or vice versa, that they do or don't like horses, tigers, elephants, mice or just about any animal you care to mention, you seldom meet a person who actually does not like swans. Even the most insensitive among us will say that somehow a swan is different. Perhaps subconsciously we are haunted by tales that they are the

91

souls of gods; or that they are the spirits of beautiful women who fled fearsome husbands. In Scotland and Ireland it is still considered unlucky to kill swans because they are believed to embody human souls. Misfortune, perhaps even death, will befall the slayer.

One myth that Len unfortunately has to dispel is that swans sing before they die. The mute swans of Britain do not, nor do they pine for each other and die from broken hearts. Len says they do grieve, and they then stop eating and become rundown. He has known them die from a kind of self-induced illness, but not from a broken heart – or perhaps within nature's laws that is the same thing.

When a swan from Mistley in Essex was critically ill at Len's home, the locals gathered together and prayed for the swan's recovery. Henry, as he was called, had severe lead-poisoning, and he died. So the locals prayed again, this time asking God not to let his lady, Henrietta, get lead-poisoning also. They loved their swans and some Mistley folk openly sobbed when they heard Henry had died.

From America, the following story came to Len of two much loved swans that lived together on a lake. The female was blind and the male would guide her as they swam everywhere together. The nearby villagers loved these swans very much. Then one morning some campers arrived at the lake, shot the blind swan, cooked it and ate it. 'A couple of hours later when word reached the village the people went berserk, and the campers quickly found themselves surrounded by an angry mob. I gather there were very soon some very hurt campers.'

Another story from America concerns a village pesonality known as Billy Blue, because he always wore blue denims. All his life he had fed the swans every day. He would stand in the reeds surrounded by his white-feathered friends and talk to them while he fed them. Then one day Billy Blue died, and the swans stopped coming. The locals say that as they were burying Billy Blue twelve white swans flew over his grave.

That man and bird could have such a bond Len accepts totally. The rest of us perhaps will go on questioning, but then we haven't had the uncanny experiences that Len has. We haven't had a swan rub its face against ours as if to say 'thank you'; we haven't been guided by one swan to another sick one. Perhaps it is only when you live so close to each other that you learn to communicate without language.

One bitterly cold winter's day Len saw a swan standing on a riverbank; an icicle had formed on its beak and was so long that it had attached itself to the bird's feathers. The swan couldn't open its beak or move its head. Left like that the creature could have starved to death. Len borrowed a dinghy, rowed over to the swan, and knowing there was only one answer to the problem he put the bird's beak into his mouth and kept it there until the ice thawed and the swan could eat again. The amazing thing is that the swan just sat patiently and waited, with its beak inside a human's mouth. As Len says, it is as if the bird understood.

But love works both ways. There aren't many of us who could put a wild bird's beak into our mouths; or sift through its faeces with a drinking straw looking for pieces of lead. Nor could many of us do what Len had to do when a swan he had got in the car suddenly collapsed.

When I'm on my own I always sit the sick swan on the front passenger seat, partly so I can keep an eye on it, but also because they love to sit there. Swans love cars, they are excellent travellers, smashing passengers, better than a dog. But they particularly like to sit in the front because they can lay their beaks over the de-mist vent, that really turns them on.

Miracle, as I eventually called her, seemed quite content, enjoying the ride, when suddenly she coughed. That worried me because I thought it meant she was going to vomit and that's something swans can't cope with, it often kills them. As I stopped the car her beak fell off the dashboard and slipped on to the floor. I grabbed her, put my ear to her chest and it seemed as though her heart had stopped beating. I didn't know what to do. I'd never lost a swan this way before, and never in the car. I panicked, and I decided there was only one thing to do. Whether it worked or not I don't know, I'll never know.

Len put his mouth over the swan's nostrils, held the beak tightly shut, and blew as hard as he could. Now as you know a swan's neck is very long, and perhaps what Len did had no effect whatsoever, but suddenly the swan's little heart was beating again. She had been given a second chance. Perhaps Len's kiss of life saved her, perhaps not: all Len can remember is that he was trembling a little as he sped back home averaging about 80 m.p.h. But, just as they were nearing Sparham, the weak head fell to the floor again. Len lifted it up, tucked it under the bird's wing to make her more comfortable, and continued on his journey.

I gave the customary two beeps on the car horn that tells Sheila we've got a serious case coming in and she's to get the operating room ready quickly. She came running out to meet us, just as she always does, and I said 'Sorry pet, we're too late for this one.' We carried Miracle into the kitchen, sat her on the table, and her head fell down the side. She seemed very dead. But for some reason I hit her on the back. I don't know what made me do that, I wouldn't normally hit a dead swan, but it had an effect, for we both detected a tiny movement. I slapped her again and for the second time it seemed she was trying to lift her head.

Sheila said, 'Hold everything.' She opened the lounge door and as usual the couple's noisy, barking, jumping, over-excited poodles, Oliver and Paddington, came bounding into the kitchen, an area that they are normally under strict orders to keep out of. And here was Sheila actually opening the door for them – they couldn't believe their luck! They circled Miracle, making a tremendous noise. They jumped up at the table she was lying on, barking and yapping in triumph. But Miracle wasn't taking that sort of treatment from two scruffy poodles. She looked up, leapt off the table and tried to attack both the dogs with her wings. The dogs had done their stuff and Sheila's trick had worked, for suddenly a very dead-looking swan was a very alive one, and kicking. Miracle was a lead victim, but Sheila and Len worked on her for a couple of months and eventually she flew back to freedom and is now one of a group of swans at King's Lynn.

It is strange that swans should like travelling in cars. They are wild birds, remember, and one would expect a small, confined space to frighten them. Having one in the car can lead to some

funny remarks though. Travelling back from Hampshire one afternoon with a diesel-damaged swan on the front seat Len got caught
in a slow-moving traffic jam near Heathrow Airport. A taxi driver
cruising past in the next lane yelled across: 'What flight's he
on?"

'Six-thirty,' yelled back Len.

'He's bloody missed it then,' came the reply. 'Where was he
going, Swansea?'

In another incident, somewhat naughtily, Len used the usual
human disbelief of seeing a swan in a car to get his own back on a
man with whom he had had some friction.

A garage owner that Len knows was notorious for his heavy
drinking. Not that Len cared about that, but very often when
buying petrol here much of it went on to the ground instead of
into the tank. Len therefore tried not to use this particular garage
– petrol is expensive for all of us, but for Len who relies on public
donations to cover these costs such a waste is next to criminal. But
as this garage is the only one in the area that is open on a Sunday,
Len is sometimes forced to fill up there. Not so long ago he drove
into the garage with a swan on the passenger's seat, looking very
perky as it gazed through the windows at the world outside. The
garage man was the worse for drink as usual.

'Excuse me,' said the man, 'did you know there's a swan in your
car?'

'You what, mate?' said Len.

'A swan, there's a swan in your car.'

'Where?'

'There!' shouted the drunk. 'A swan, on your front seat,'

'You feeling all right?'

'There's a swan in your car,' said the man, becoming more and
more red in the face.

'I don't want to get personal,' said Len, having great trouble in
keeping a straight face, 'but do you drink?'

Grabbing his change Len got into the car and left. The man
stood on the forecourt scratching his head.

A while later Len had to call in again at the garage and this time
the wife served him. 'I don't know what you said to my husband,'
she said, 'but he hasn't touched a drop of drink since you last came
here.'

Swan love or affection cannot be taken for granted: swans can be as fickle as humans, and when they have decided they don't like something or someone they make their feelings clear. Len has a friend, an engineer in the boatyard where he used to work, who for some inexplicable reason has a swan enemy. Jack Wythes is over six foot tall, a strong, good-hearted, no-nonsense sort of man. He is kind to swans and wouldn't dream of hurting one. Jack was often called to work on boats in the marina at Yarmouth, and there lives a flock of swans. For some reason one of these swans does not like Jack. And he certainly made his feelings obvious! At first Len did not believe Jack; swans don't take personal dislikes, Len thought. But then Jack had another incident with this swan. He was in an inflatable boat, working behind the engine of a large cruiser, and there were holidaymakers on the quayside watching. Suddenly Jack heard the dreaded hissing. 'Oh no, not you,' he thought. It was the same swan. He had seen Jack in his water, so he had left the flock and come to deal with him. He got Jack's ankle in his beak and wouldn't let go until Jack got out of the inflatable and back on dry land. Jack was simply not allowed in this possessive swan's water! Poor Jack had to finish preparing the engine by leaning over from the top of the cruiser and working upside down, out of the swan's reach. Jack went straight to Len with news of this latest event, with proof this time, for the holidaymakers had witnessed it. Even so, Len couldn't understand why the swan should have anything against Jack. Jack, though worried, agreed with Len; a gentle man, he had never hurt a swan, had never even shouted at one.

The next time Jack went to Yarmouth he cast off his usual blue overalls and wore a different colour, left behind the pipe he always smokes, and put on a woolly hat. But sure enough, as soon as the swan spied Jack he left the flock and came over. Jack now tries to avoid Yarmouth, and Len has been forced to accept that for some curious reason there is something about Jack that this swan doesn't like.

Another strange incident was to occur not long after Jack's experiences, this time concerning not just one swan but many. Len was in desperate need of some extra pairs of hands to help with the swans in the garden. It had been a particularly busy period and he had put out word among his friends that anyone with a few spare hours to offer would be greatly welcomed.

A very nice, very presentable young man came round. He was interested in the work we were doing, he obviously liked swans, and he wanted to help. I was delighted and we agreed that he would take over the feeding. I took him to the pens to show him what to do and every swan, forty-two in all, retreated to the furthest corner and stared at him. I thought that perhaps it was his red jacket, so he went away, took it off, and came back, but again they all walked to the furthest corner away from him. They all gazed at him, not moving. He'd done nothing to hurt them, on the contrary he wanted to help, but there was something about him they just didn't like. He couldn't help me; the swans wouldn't accept him, it was as simple as that.

Vesta and Benjy were to carve themselves a place for ever in Len and Sheila's hearts. They were both terribly ill. Vesta had been shot and Benjy was nearly dead from lead-poisoning. The swans hadn't known each other before they arrived at Len's, but they became devoted friends, living together in their own pen. But despite getting priority treatment and nursing they were both in a critical condition.

When a swan is very ill the kindest thing often is to allow it to die. This is a hard decision for Len to make, but it is even crueller, he thinks, to keep a swan lingering on when there is no hope for it. He has a system which he calls the 'death date': making a judgement on the swan's condition and how it should respond, he marks a day in the diary with a circle with a cross in it. The 'death date' for both Vesta and Benjy was 30 June. If they were not on the mend by then he would have to ask the vet to put them to sleep.

Every day Len and Sheila would go to Vesta and Benjy hoping to see improvement, but no, the two swans never seemed to be picking up. The dreaded date got nearer and nearer. On the morning of 30 June they were called out very early to a rescue in King's Lynn. They returned home in silence, both knowing what had to be done on their return. It wouldn't be so hard if they did not love their swans, but each one becomes a dear friend, and to have them put down, even when they know it is the best thing, breaks their hearts. They got back to the house and went to the swans' pen. And Vesta and Benjy were side by side, snuggling close together, dead. As Len says, it was as if they were saying, 'You needn't do it, we'll do it ourselves.'

It's moments like that which really choke me: such dignity. They know when their life is over, they know when it's time for them to die. They don't make a fuss about it like humans, they don't make an agony of death, they don't make an agony of anything; they're always serene, beautiful and calm . . . and that's how they die too.

Even when a swan is undergoing an operation it will just sit and let you work on it. I used to think they were docile because they were in a state of shock but I've come to realize that isn't so. They are just elegant. They feel pain, I've known them flinch and I've known them cry, great big tears tumbling from their eyes, but they never lose their dignity.

Perhaps the most horrendous operation Len can recall was on a swan called Zarba whom he had rescued from a very heavily fished area called Potter Heigham. Zarba had two hooks in his tongue and one in his cheek. It took one hour ten minutes to remove them, and Zarba sat quietly still all the time.

He sobbed gently from time to time but he went through the operation beautifully. We'll never know the level of pain they can take, but they accept it. They are the most incredible patients, but what I can't stand is the gratitude. I don't want them being grateful for the help I've given them, I don't want them to be so friendly, to say 'thank you' in the many ways that they find to say it. I want them to remember they are wild, magnificent birds, and I'd be happier if, when I'd finished working on them, they got off the table and beat the hell out of me. Being friendly, going up to humans, swimming around boats, lingering near riverbanks is what injures and kills them. I want them to stop being so blimmin' friendly. I'd like to take all the swans off our rivers and put them back in wild places, away from humanity, where they will be safe.

Len considers himself to be the luckiest person in the world. That a wild bird has accepted him, has allowed him into its world, overwhelms him.

It's a precious gift, to be allowed by a bird to enter his environment to learn his ways, to understand his needs, to get to know his personality, his joys and fears. I sometimes can't believe it has all happened to me, but I know deep down that it was meant to happen. In the process it is teaching me to be a better human being, at least I hope it is. The swan has taught me, more than any human, basic ingredients of civilization. He's taught me implicit and utter truth, for that's what a swan is. He is what he is. He does what he does. He doesn't know about deceit or lying. He doesn't bear malice. He's never jealous or envious. He has nothing in his life except freedom and the sky. He has taught me to prefer looking at a copper beech than a colour telly. He's taught me to smell the air, touch the grass, drink the river water. He's taught me that these are the important things in life, not possessions and all the other man-made trappings that we call civilization.

A swan is never greedy. He needs food but he'll never over-eat. He takes what he needs but no more. I think that's what I'm learning from swans, not to want more than I need. I need food and shelter. I also want stimulating conversation and I couldn't live without Mahler; I cheat a little but I'm human, I'm not perfect like a swan.

But I'm struggling to throw off the human way of looking at things. I've no real concept of time any more, I just know whether it's day or night. We don't bother with birthdays any more, or the commerical trappings of events like Easter and Christmas. Except that people send me cards and tell me they are from the swans and the funny thing is I believe them.

When he began in 1977 Len was frightened, he admits that now. He would sit for hours wondering if he was doing the right thing. Should he get so involved with the swans? But looking back now he says the decision never was his, it was the swans'.

They made the decision for us, we just did as they requested. And they've put us through it, Sheila and I. We lost our furniture and our money. They've pushed us to extremes of physical and mental tiredness – there have been days when we thought we'd break in two – but there was never any question of us stopping. The swans cast their spell over us; we did what they wanted, and we always will. In return they've helped us get our priorities right, they've taught us to be better people, and how can we ever thank them for that?

Loyalty is strong within a swan's personality, which sometimes leads to incongruous moments, for while it is true that they will fight each other to the death to protect their territory they will also fight alongside each other against a common enemy.

A swan on a loch in Scotland was in trouble and the scene was witnessed by some holidaymakers who passed on the story to Len. Something was grabbing at the swan's foot; Len presumes it was a pike, for they are known to attack swans, and especially cygnets. The swan was struggling, unable to see and deal with the attacker which was encircling it beneath the water. Another swan arrived on the scene, stopped for a few seconds, summed up the situation and then to the onlookers' surprise flew away, as if abandoning its friend. But within minutes the sky was full of swans. A flock, some thirty or forty, swooped down to assist their fellow swan. They landed on the loch and began to beat the water with their wings. This presumably frightened the pike, for very quickly the distressed swan's flipper was released and they all flew away together.

Len lives on stories like this. They are life and breath to him, for ever deepening his love of swans. At his breaking points, those moments when he feels he can't cope any more, something always happens – a story like that or a little dab of swan magic that lifts his spirits to get him through to another dawn. One such event took place on the open, bleak marshes of Norfolk. Len had received a report that a cygnet had been seen with a drooping wing. It was a filthy day: solid, relentless rain and a low, threatening sky. But out Len and Sheila went, together as usual, to search for a tiny cygnet in a vast marshland. They were tired before they started; very soon they were wet and cold, on the verge of depression and collapse.

Luck was on their side, for they found the cygnet quite quickly and enticed it with bread. But it wasn't playing. It didn't want to know about bread games, and it walked away. Len and Sheila followed. The faster they walked, the more the cygnet gathered speed. They chased it for a long while in the slippery, sopping wet marsh. Eventually they got it cornered in a dyke. As Len now says, frustrating situations make you do silly things, and he was definitely silly. This non-swimmer, who is scared of water, threw himself into the dyke in the direction of the cygnet. As he landed in the icy water the cygnet side-stepped, looked at him as if to say 'you stupid idiot', and walked up the bank and out of sight.

I got out of the water soaking wet – not that it mattered for I was wet before. Sheila was also drenched. We were cold and frightened, the rain was streaming down our faces, our hair was stuck to our heads, and suddenly it all seemed so funny. We just burst out laughing and threw ourselves backwards into the reeds like a couple of kids. We were covered in filth and mud, our clothes were drenched and we just lay there under the rain. We couldn't have been wetter, but what the hell! We closed our eyes and felt the rain landing on our faces, it was wonderful.

We could hear our own hearts thumping as we lay there looking up at the magnificent sky. We hadn't been to bed the night before. It was the first time we'd lain down in 48 hours; we were exhausted and lying there was paradise. We were just thinking about going home when suddenly Sheila told me very quietly to look down past my feet. And there, after three and a half hours of chasing him, the little cygnet had come and sat with us in the rain. He was by my feet and looking at us as if to say what game shall we play now?

This playful ten-month-old had hit a power cable and wounded his wing, but he was all right, so Len and Sheila kissed him goodbye and thanked him for the experience.

They returned home wet through but with their hearts full of joy again. All depression had been swept aside by the little cygnet who, like every swan this couple meet, had made them fall in love with him.

Releasing

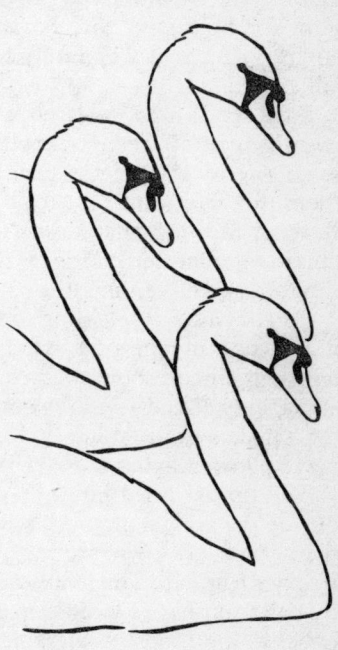

It overwhelms me
That you return my friendship.
I wish you wouldn't.
It is flattering
To know you love me
In your own way.
I wish you didn't.
For you are a wild spirit
And a free spirit
And must remain so
To survive.
It will hurt me
When you leave,
But it would hurt more
Should you begin
To accept human friendship,
And then to be betrayed
By some other human.
Forgive me if our goodbye
Gets clouded with
Misty eyes.
I am after all
Only human
And you, after all
Are a swan.
Goodbye swan.

Release days have their own poignancy for Len and Sheila. By the
time a swan is fit again and ready to fly back to freedom he or she

has become one of the family. Even the slightest injury will normally necessitate a swan remaining at their home for a couple of weeks; some of course will have been with them for many months.

Saying goodbye is sad for two reasons. A friend is going, a little personality that allowed itself to be held, to be touched and befriended is looking at the sky with eagerness. Its wounds healed and morale back to peak condition, it is anxious to get away. Len is happy to give the swans their freedom, and it is a rewarding moment in his work. But there is another reason why it upsets him, for he knows that he is putting his friends back into an environment that will surely hurt them again, or next time even kill them.

Last April Len released a batch of 65 swans; within four months over 50 were back with him or known to be dead. As he says, one of his biggest problems is knowing where to release them, for safe water, especially in East Anglia, is at a premium. Bearing in mind that swans can live to fifty years of age, it is horrifying that Len considers the average lifespan in Norfolk to be three years and ten months.

Len has a strict releasing procedure. When the bird is ready, be it just one or one of a batch, he is put on the kitchen table, weighed, checked over, given a final dose of worming medicine and a farewell meal. All the details are recorded. A survival weight for a male swan is about 26 lb, for a female about 21 lb; they are never allowed to leave under these weights.

The timing must be right, too, for they must not be released during the annual moult. Nature has been very clever here. When the cygnets are born, around June or July, the female will start to lose her feathers. The moult takes six to eight weeks, which means that the mother is unable to fly and therefore cannot leave her babes at their most vulnerable time. She is there to protect them from predators while the male is away hunting for food. As her moult ends, the male's begins and he is then unable to fly. The cygnets therefore always have one or other parent with them when they most need protection.

To release a swan during its moult, when it cannot fly away from danger should it need to, would be cruel and indeed stupid. Len therefore may have to decide whether to hurry up a treatment and perhaps release a swan a little before he might otherwise have done, or else keep the swan confined to his garden for some weeks longer than might have been necessary. Always, what is best for the swan is what counts. When you have got over a hundred swans in your garden, plus cygnets in your kitchen, your own convenience or otherwise has already become irrelevant. The Bakers' home serves swans. They stay as long as necessary, they are admitted when necessary – there is no waiting list for beds at this hospital.

Len's car will hold about ten swans. When there are more birds than that to be released a convoy of friends' cars can be seen making its way to the releasing point. The swans travel in a specially designed harness made of soft fabric; this is wrapped around the swan's body, rather like a strait-jacket, so that it won't damage its wings during the journey. Being good passengers they very often go to sleep, and as corners are turned all necks sway in one direction then straighten up again.

Uncannily, the swans will become alert when water is near. Even if it is dark and the water can't be seen, or perhaps the car is going over a bridge, heads will twitch and necks will crane to look out of the window. Perhaps they can smell the water, who knows; they can certainly tell when they are in its vicinity.

Once at their destination another procedure is followed. The releasing points are carefully selected by Len, who refuses to put swans into areas that are fished or polluted or have inadequate vegetation. He is adamant about this, and thereby causes himself many problems for such ideal places are rare. Sometimes he is offered access to private lakes, but again the same standard of safety has to be met although he does now have a list of safe swan homes.

The swans are all marked with numbered rings and are released in numerical order. Once out of their travelling jackets the birds stretch their limbs, have a good look round and usually waddle straight into the water. Sometimes they need some encouragement and a little pat on their bottoms, but usually they go straight in and away.

Zorba, despite his one-time angry attack on Len, was one of the swans who had obviously become a little too attached to his cosy home. He had spent three weeks in the Bakers' garden after they had removed a fish-hook from his cheek, and when it came to releasing him he kept flying back to their red car. Each time Len and Sheila had returned to where they had parked the car Zorba would be ahead of them and standing by the passenger door waiting to go home again. When he did finally go he flew a lap of honour around their heads, as if to say thank you.

But normally the swans, especially the mature birds, are eager to get back into the water and taste freedom again, although it is obvious that they are having to readjust to a vast expanse of water after the small pools they have become used to in Len's garden. Sometimes the bold birds will fly immediately, eager to soar into the sky again; others will explore the river and bathe before flying.

Watching them fly away is sometimes too moving for words. Sheila and I used to wait and watch them all go, but we don't now, it's too much to bear. We can't speak to each other; anyway all words seem redundant, there's nothing that is adequate to explain how you feel at that moment.

A part of me flies away with them, I'm up there with them in the sky, free and happy. They are so innocent, they've no idea of the dangers that surround them and in a way that makes me feel a traitor. I can't keep them for ever, I have to let them go back to the wild, but I do it knowing they live in peril. We're filled with happiness and heartbreak all at the same time, we're too choked to talk.

Back in the car the couple drive home in silence. Swan friends have gone; Len hopes they know that he loves them and that he wishes them well. He pushes to the back of his mind the ever-favourable odds that he will be seeing them again.

A batch of twelve swans was to be released one lovely autumn morning and Len, always in need of public donations, had informed the local newspaper in the hope of getting some publicity. The release time was scheduled for 10 o'clock, but no photographer arrived and the swans were getting restless in their jackets. They could see the water and they wanted to be in it. Eventually Len decided he could wait no longer and the lucky swans were off to freedom. Just as they merged as block dots in

106

the sky a panting newspaper photographer appeared on the scene. 'Sorry I'm late, can you call them back and release them again?'

Power over swans is something that even Len does not have and he was unable to oblige the young man, who seemed somewhat surprised. Len's reputation, it seemed, was not only going before him, it was getting somewhat distorted in the process. Swans, he explained, weren't like dogs; they didn't come to heel when he whistled.

Indeed not. In fact the full problems of releasing, and the delicacies surrounding the operation, were again taught to Len and Sheila by the swans themselves. And as usual it was a case of trial and error, with the swans letting them know if they got it wrong. One bad mistake they made could have been tragic, but the swans involved, as Len maintains they always do, guided him.

It was a bad mistake, probably the worst I've ever made, but you live and learn. I'd put the wrong numbered rings on the wrong swans and in the process I'd separated a pair. I released the male first; he was fine, and straight away he flew right up into the sky, probably unaware that his lady wasn't behind him. But I'd got her 14 swans down the line and she watched him go. She cried as loudly as she could when she realized he was flying away. She put her head up and made an incredible noise, I'd never heard anything like it. She realized he was going without her, that they were being separated.

We knew immediately what we had done. We rushed to her, took off her harness and she went straight into the water. But we were panicking, for he had flown in one direction and she was swimming in the other. We didn't know what to do. About eight minutes passed and we thought we'd separated them for good. She was still making her incredible cry. She was calling to him, crying out in great despair. Then suddenly there was a noise in the sky above our heads – he'd come back for her. He circled over her slowly as she swam in the river and he called to her. She took off and they met in the sky. We saw them speak to each other, then they turned left and flew out towards the sea together. They never looked back. They'd gone.

Len and Sheila sighed with relief: to have been responsible for separating a loving pair would have broken their hearts. But all was well, and the experience taught them to check ring numbers more thoroughly in future.

There are some difficult situations, however, that the Bakers have no hand in nor can they do anything about. Sometimes injured cygnets come to them so young that they have not yet been taught to fly; some of them have only just learned to swim, let alone fly. Once a cygnet has been away from its parents for a while they won't accept it back again, so the poor youngster has no instructor. And cygnets do have to be taught to fly. While flying itself is second nature to them, they have to learn the mechanics of it from their parents. As with aeroplanes, it is the taking off and landing that are particularly difficult, and this is not something a human can teach them.

Solo was one such cygnet. At three weeks old he had been injured with a fish-hook in his throat. At that age he was still fluffy and his wings hadn't even developed. He recovered slowly from his injury, and was five months old before he could be released. With no guidance from his parents, he had to rely totally on instinct. Len hoped it wouldn't let Solo down, and he was full of trepidation as he carried the little swan to the river.

Len put him on the water's edge and he paddled away with the other swans which were being released with him. And then, in what Len calls one of those magical swan moments, he turned and faced the wind, paddled upstream, opened his wings and soared like a professional.

Up he went against the wind and he played like a child with a new toy. He went round and round playing in the wind. We counted eight laps, and then he decided to land, and it was panic stations. You didn't have to read anything into his actions: you could see from his face it had suddenly dawned on him he didn't know how to land. Half-way down he was thinking, 'How the hell do I do it?'

We'd assumed that swans just knew how to land, but they don't, and you could see that this little creature was frightened. He came down and held out his little flippers but he was going much too fast and at completely the wrong angle. I dread to think at what speed he hit the water. He didn't even fold his

108

wings in time and he tumbled head over heels; he did three somersaults – he didn't know where he was.

A very shaken Solo soon regained his dignity. When he came to his senses he folded his wings up properly, brushed himself down and tried to look as if to say, 'I was just giving you something to smile at.' Then he paddled upstream and had another go: he took off for the second time. 'They've got their flight plan in their brain. It's very complicated and little Solo had to practise. Considering he'd had no instructions he was really very brave. At least he'd learned one important thing from his practice run: he'd got to fold his wings immediately on touch-down.'

This time Solo got everything right. His dive breaks went out at the right time, legs at the right angle, neck forward, contact, wings in – a perfect landing. Sadly his experience of flight was brief. Five months later he was found dead: another victim of lead-poisoning, another post-mortem statistic.

The swans' most precious possession, indeed their only possession, is what Len calls their God-given right – freedom. And when a swan leaves the water and goes to the sky Len feels that he too is truly touching freedom, and perhaps thus understanding something of a swan's experience.

As a swan soars upwards it elates my heart – not just the beauty, not just because it's a friend of mine up there, but to be with him, just for a second in time, soaring upwards, shrugging off man-made responsibilities and problems. To be able to take to the sky is nature's gift to them, and that they allow me to be a part of that, that they share it with me, is their gift to me. And I can never thank them enough. I feel I've said to this bird, 'There's your river again, there's your sky.' I'm saying sorry on behalf of mankind for the pain and suffering we've given them; or at least, I'm trying to.

Len is not ashamed to admit that he often weeps as he watches the swans fly away. 'I'm sometimes filled with an emptiness I can't describe. A piece of me goes with every swan I release. I'll be with them for ever, even the swans that die never leave me.'

*   *   *

109

Len is often asked by members of the public if he will sell them a swan. His answer is an emphatic 'No'. He doesn't sell swans for he doesn't consider them his to sell, nor does he consider that a swan is a piece of retailing merchandise. 'I've been offered £500 for a pair of breeding swans but I don't want it, no matter how badly I need the money. To sell a swan would make me as guilty as the people who run wildlife parks. As far as I'm concerned making money out of wild birds or animals is evil.'

He will though, on occasion, give a swan to genuine swan-lovers, for their lake or pond. He is very particular about whom he gives them to and checks the conditions the swan will live in before parting with it, but if he is happy that the people really care for swans he will allow them to have one of his convalescing birds once it is strong enough. What is best for the swan always comes first in Len's calculations, and some of his ex-patients now live in very grand surroundings.

Some people phone up and think we're running a swan shop. They ask for a swan, preferably white, to be delivered on so-and-so day. I've got a stock answer for them! Others ask more tactfully but when you talk it over with them you can sense they want the bird to add value to their property. They want to be able to show off to the guests as they sip cocktails and gaze at 'the swan' through the french windows. Those kind of people are quickly put off when I tell them the work involved. It hadn't occurred to them that swans have to be looked after. That you have to get up at the crack of dawn in the winter and break the ice for them.

Genuine homes are hard to come by, but they do crop up. Many people, especially substantial landowners with private lakes, have offered their facilities to Len's swans, and on occasion Len has been grateful to accept. He is happy to know that at least some of his swans have safe, private homes away from boating, anglers and lead.

We've shocked a few people, though. Sheila and I go and inspect the lake. It must be at least 3½-4 feet deep with good vegetation and no pollution. We sip the water and we taste the reeds. The people stare at us as though we are mad but we don't care; I'm not putting my swans anywhere that isn't just right. If the gardener uses pesticides or herbicides near the lake I tell them that must stop or I won't leave the swans with them.

Buried six foot down in Len's garden are 198 swans, for in the days before every swan was given a post-mortem he used to bury them when they died. He assumes he has probably broken some law or other, but swans were dying daily and he didn't know what else to do with them.

One such little swan was Marlon's daughter Paulette. Len had rescued her from near her home on the River Bure, but the fish-hook in her windpipe killed her within twenty-four hours. She was just eight months old. She died in Sheila's arms, cuddling-up like the baby that she was.

Like all the swans in those days, little Paulette was given the Indian bird funeral that Len had been taught by his North American Indian friends earlier in his life. Ironically Paulette's burial was held on a Friday 13th, a clear, crisp Norfolk March morning. Once her little grave had been dug Sheila and Len held her body to the sky, released one of her breast feathers to the wind and together said the words: 'White Spirit, fly free.' That, according to the Indians, releases the bird's spirit from its body and gives it eternal life and freedom. Then the body was laid in the ground, a pillow of grass under its head, and covered with lime and earth.

Len no longer buries his swans, for he considers that the scientific evidence that can be obtained from post-mortems is vital and much needed in the long-term struggle to save the birds. But that does not mean that he has stopped praying for them, although his prayer these days is that these magnificient birds should be free from man-made dangers and be able to fly safely wherever their spirit chooses to take them. White spirits, he says, have the right to fly free.

Swan Rescue Today

Did we do right
A thousand pains ago?
Should we have left you
Upon your river of indifference?
We are glad
We interfered and chased a dream.
We only hope our dream was your dream.
We think it was.
And we will never awaken from it.

Castelnaudary is a small town in south-west France and it was to the peace and tranquillity of this area that Len and Sheila were banished in the summer of 1982. Len had not been feeling well. He had been experiencing double vision, and then one morning, after several nights of next to no sleep, he had a minor collapse. He just sat on the ground and thought he saw the walls flying in the air above him. His body was telling him that enough was enough: it needed a rest, and if he wasn't going to let up voluntarily, it would force him to.

After much persuasion and nagging from friends, the couple packed a few things and drove to France. It was the first holiday they had had together since they began Swan Rescue, indeed it was the first time they had even given themselves a few days off.

Needless to say they didn't stop thinking about swans. On the canal that runs through the small town of Castelnaudary live some swans and Len couldn't help noticing one afternoon that one of them was looking very sorry for herself with her tail down in the water, a sure sign that she was unwell. He went over and called to her, and she came immediately and allowed Len to lift her out of the water. A cursory examination on the canalside confirmed that she was sick, but Len couldn't be sure what the trouble was. With the intention of finding a vet he picked up the swan, and with it tucked under his arm he and Sheila walked along the town's main street. Within minutes they were surrounded by local residents. Unable to speak French, Len couldn't explain who he was or what he was doing. 'They poked and prodded us – we were very frightened. They obviously thought we were stealing their swan, and like people everywhere they were very possessive about their swans. I didn't know what to do. The swan needed help but on the other hand these people looked as though they were going to lynch us.'

As always, fate stepped in, and an Australian man whom Len had got friendly with earlier and who spoke French helped to explain the situation. The angry crowd backed down, but they were still puzzled and not totally convinced. Len and Sheila were being regarded with great suspicion. The town hall was contacted and word came back that every assistance was to be given to this couple from England. The vet was to do what Len requested and his bill would be met out of town hall funds. 'The vet was brilliant. I told him what three drugs I needed and he had them. He watched while I did the injections, and just kept saying "*bon, bon*".'

The swan's problem was a very bad case of worms. She had had an earlier injury which the vet had seen to but no one had given the Baker after-op care and nursing, and back on the water she had become extremely run down. With the townsfolk watching Len carried the swan back to the canal, and many eager witnesses watched as their swan was placed back where she belonged. And still the residents of Castelnaudary wonder how Swan Rescue, England, knew that their little swan was ill and why they bothered to travel all that way to treat her.

Swan Rescue is indeed a far cry now from those early days of the late seventies. The Bakers' network of contacts has built up, their knowledge has increased dramatically and their reputation has grown. They have not yet got contacts in small European towns, but it's on Len's schedule!

Expansion is constantly in his mind, but of course it demands money, and Len has little of that. At the time of writing Swan

Rescue costs over £300 a week to run, and nearly all of this comes from public donations.

They receive little help from authorities. The Royal Society for the Protection of Birds does not give grants, and requests for money have been refused by various other bodies, including the RSPCA and the World Wildlife Fund (the latter told me that as they have limited finances themselves they do not consider Len's work to be a sufficient conservation priority). The Broads Authority gave Len a grant of £800 in 1981 with the promise of a further £200 a year for three years, but that represents the sum total of all the help the Bakers have received from officialdom.

Everything else is given by individuals, among them members of the Royal Family – including the Queen Mother, whose unexpected cheque helped Len to pay a long outstanding vet's bill.

The biggest expense is the running of the four Swan Rescue cars, each averaging about 1,000 miles a week at a cost of £80 each in petrol alone; car repairs in one twelve-month period came to just over £2,000. Len asks a lot of his cars, which he expects to fly down motorways and perform like army tanks on marshland. Wheels three-foot deep in mud are a common occurrence, and he remembers with some humour now, although he didn't think it funny at the time, the occasion when the car turned sideways into a four-foot hole, water was seeping into the interior and the breakdown company wouldn't assist unless Len had £25 cash on him. He hadn't. So a friend had to drive to him with the money first, then the breakdown truck came to his aid. That particular adventure took all day, and at the end of it the car, and the Bakers, were caked in mud. When seven months later that car, their fourth, finally and literally went bang, Len was advised by the garage not to spend any more money on it. He is now on his fifth car in six years.

Another major and vital expense is treatment for the swans. X-rays, drugs and vets' skills are all very expensive. There are many aspects of treatment that Len can now do himself, especially on the diagnostic side. It is seldom these days he cannot identify a swan's illness, and once he knows what is wrong he is very often able to treat it himself. But this is a tricky area, for not being a qualified veterinary surgeon he is not supposed to perform oper-

114

ations or to be in possession of certain drugs. He has to tread a tight-rope between staying within the law and saving swans' lives. He readily admits that time and circumstance, on occasion, have forced him to do things that perhaps legally he should not, but if he has saved a swan's life in the process that is all that matters to him. Strictly speaking he should not cut into a bird or amputate, but if it is 3 o'clock in the morning and a swan is bleeding to death, which has happened to him on more than one occasion, Len maintains that the situation demands a correct sense of priorities. He has learnt how to do surgery and how to amputate from spending many hours beside vets watching them at work; he also knows how to administer anaesthetic.

At present he has the assistance of a local vet – 'a truly wonderful man', says Len, for he is prepared to be called out at all hours and does not charge Len punitive fees. For the time being therefore Len doesn't have to tangle with the law, but if this vet were to move or become too busy for Len's constant flow of demanding patients he would be back in his predicament.

The laws that Len is dodging in and out of are concerned with cruelty to the animal, qualifications within veterinary surgery and the possession of certain drugs, especially anaesthetic and eutha-nasia drugs.

The many people to whom I have spoken in veterinary and animal welfare circles feel that Len's reputation, dedication and, most important of all, his results, would be sufficient defence were anyone to prosecute him.

In 1981 he did have a scare. He was informed that the RSPCA were going to prosecute him and they made an inspection of his home and garden. He heard no more from them. I spoke with the RSPCA head office during the writing of this book and it was confirmed to me that prosecution of Len Baker had been considered but that the inspection of his property and the swans had dispelled their anxieties. The RSPCA would not be prosecut-ing, I was told.

Len is able to do injections and stitch up wounds; he deals with other injuries and administers many drugs. He cannot do X-rays for he doesn't yet have the facilities, although he intends to buy his own X-ray machine when he can raise the money. In the meantime he has to pay £10 per X-ray.

The drugs he administers himself he does, of course, have to buy. Antibiotic injections, for example, are a routine daily treatment. A 100 ml bottle of the drug costs £6, providing up to 50 injections; it will last Len about one week. The soluble anitibiotic that he puts in the swans' drinking water is £13 a tub; he buys one of those every fortnight. The locally applied antibiotic that comes in a squeezer cost £1 and he uses about one a day for most of the year.

The worming drug is just over £30 for a 500 ml bottle which lasts three months. The drug for the treatment of his lead-poisoned swans costs about £6.50 per 100 ml bottle which provides some 25 injections. He averages 25 injections every two to three days.

All the swans that come under his care, regardless of what is wrong with them, are given vitamins. Many need them on arrival, others which are confined to his garden for some weeks need them because away from their natural environment they can become run down. Vitamim B12 which he puts in their drinking water to give them an appetite costs about 50p a day; a multi-vitamin and mineral powder, also for their drinking water, costs £9 a week.

Despite being able to do most of the treatments himself visits to the vet, or the vet's visits to him, are still inevitable and expensive. The amputation of a wing costs about £25; and the one fish-hook removal that Len will not do himself, a hook in the windpipe, costs about £15.

All the prices quoted here have VAT added to them which Len, not having a business with a turnover of at least £17,000, is unable to reclaim. This is a sore point with him, for he considers he is providing a service that should not have to be provided in the first place and then being taxed for the privilege.

The third major expense is the swans' food. They need corn, or grain of some kind, plus greens – cabbage leaves, sprouts, lettuce, whichever can be obtained at the cheapest price. Because they lack dry storage space they cannot buy in bulk, so Sheila drives every day to buy a couple of hundred weight of corn; the cost of grain alone amounts to about £460 a fortnight at £3.95 per 26 lb bag. Even when in season lettuces cost about 20p each and during the summer Sheila buys four dozen a day. Lettuce is particularly good for growing cygnets; the adult swans love them too, but cost

116

forbids such luxuries.

A restaurant in Norwich has given the Bakers permission to go through its dustbins, a task which often yields cast-off greens such as sprouts and cabbages; if the swans are really in luck they may get a taste of broccoli, or even asparagus.

Finally the telephone bill. This has increased steadily with the growing reputation of Swan Rescue, and is currently about £1,000 a year. As Len says, he and Sheila have no social life, so this massive bill is entirely attributable to swan business.

If the Swan Rescue Service is to stay in business it has to raise at least £16,000 a year at current prices. On top of that Len and Sheila have to live. Their rent is very low and has not been increased in the six years they have been at the cottage. When the swan rescuing work began Len mentioned to the landlord that he and Sheila might be getting one or two birds, and the landlord replied that he didn't mind. But as Len admits, no one had any idea that one or two would turn out to be one or two hundred! Fortunately the landlord is tolerant, indeed he has been very kind: he is a farmer, and on one occasion delivered two tons of barley to Len at no cost.

The heating in the cottage is minimal. The Bakers will not light a fire because jackdaws live in the chimney, so the only source of heat is a small electric fire. The bedrooms and bathroom remain unheated. A hot meal at the end of each day and plenty of hot coffee during the day keep them going through the most bitter weather. Their personal outgoings are thus very small.

Len still manages to do some painting, despite the over-tiredness and shortage of daylight hours. Some nights he spends sketching and painting; his subject matter is always swans, and he can sell his pictures for between £60 and £100. The winter months often find the Bakers giving Women's Institute lectures. Some weeks Len will do four of these, and they earn the swans £15 an evening.

But donations from the public are the backbone of the Swan Rescue Service; without them the work could not continue. This is an incongruous situation, in which the generosity of a few people attempts to make up for the damage inflicted upon a helpless species by mankind. While Len may have become embittered towards humanity as a whole, he acknowledges that it is the support and encouragement of some people that has inspired him to carry on his work.

From the several thousands of pounds that poured in following an article about his work in a national magazine, to the odd pound note that is often thrust into his hand by a dewy-eyed onlooker who sees him doing a rescue, every penny that Len receives goes on the swans. His administration is next to nil, he has no paid staff, no expensive office. He guarantees that not a penny is wasted, and that all donations go into the swans' own bank account at the Midland Bank in Norwich. The sore-footed, kind-hearted people of Suffolk who in July 1982 raised £1,100 on a sponsored walk will no doubt be delighted to hear this. So too will the ten-year-old schoolboy who rowed all alone on a Norfolk Broad for many hours and raised £40 in sponsorship for the swans. Then there were the soldiers at Colchester who held a sponsored high-speed shave and raised £35; the local cub scouts who raised £100 in one year; and the Newmarket schoolchildren who raised £250. When a British magazine article about Len and Sheila was syndicated to Australia a donation of £30 arrived from the Sunday School children of Sydney Cathedral.

Children figure largely in Len's fund-raising, for they are often the keenest to walk miles, to swim, sing, or do anything to help raise money for the swans. He receives swan pictures and pieces of poetry from infant schools all over the country; sometimes the letters contain their pocket money too. One little girl living on the Isle of Man sent him 35p in cash and was charged 28p in postage. Other children write to Len telling him of the swans near their homes: how they are, when their cygnets are born, what they have called them, and so on.

One woman in Liverpool, on seeing a magazine feature about Len, wrote to him but explained that she could send no money for she was an unmarried mother. She said that she was in a state of severe depression, feeling that she had nothing to live for, but that reading about the suffering of the swans had helped her get her troubles into perspective. 'I dressed up my kid,' she wrote, 'and went window shopping. We had the time of our lives. I'd wanted to end it all but your swans have given me something to live for.' That note was worth a million pounds to Len, and people like that young mother will never know how they have given strength to

Len in his darkest moments.

Pensioners too have touched Len's heart. One old lady put a little bit aside every week from her pension and sent Swan Rescue £100. And a Dunkirk veteran wrote saying that he had experienced the brutality of killing, had seen his friends blown up in front of his eyes, but had never cried until he read about the swans and their suffering. He has become a regular donor.

A donation arrives every three months from Wormwood Scrubs: a prisoner sends £4 from his wages and often includes a note to Len about the birds that appear in the prison compound.

Last summer a friend of Len's built a replica of a vintage steam engine and offered it as first prize in a raffle. The event was organized by one of the boating companies near their home and Len and Sheila were invited to draw the winning ticket. A crowd had gathered to watch the draw when slowly they became aware that there were some unexpected onlookers: all the swans on the nearby river had walked up out of the water and were watching too. A press photographer turned to Len and said: 'How did you fix that?' Whether the swans realized it or not the raffle raised them £650. A very happy Len and Sheila made for home. 'We'd only been gone about five minutes when we got a message that a swan had been hooked at the very place we'd just come from. We turned round and went straight back; it was one of the swans who'd been watching the raffle.' The crowd had not yet dispersed and many people saw an unscheduled rescue. The hook was removed and the swan was all right.

The main single fund-raiser is the newsletter that Len sends out about twice a year. This is a practice that started four years ago: then he had 12 readers, now his mailing list runs to 8,000. Len writes the letter and another friend of the swans designs it. The printing cost is about £300, but on top of this are the 8,000 stamps. The newsletter is sent, free of charge, to all swan-lovers who indicate that they would like to receive it. The project has mushroomed beyond belief, but it raises about £3,000 a year in donations – one year £5,000.

Stationery, and those 8,000 envelopes in particular, would be a problem but for the fact that an anonymous well-wisher sends,

119

every fortnight, a large brown envelope full of new, smaller-sized envelopes. There is never a covering letter, but the donation is greatly appreciated. So too are the mysterious sacks of wheat that appear from time to time at Len's gate. Never a noise of footsteps or a car is heard, but suddenly there the sack will be. It is a lovely mystery and a lovely gift.

Blankets, feeding bowls, even surgical instruments also arrive occasionally; again, with no accompanying letter. Many people like to give anonymously, especially those sending money. One donation arrives regularly from Scotland: always £7 in Scottish notes and always with the accompanying message, 'From the North'.

The largest anonymous donation, indeed the largest single donation Len has ever had, was given in 1981. A radio firm in Norwich contacted Len and told him to take his car into them. They had received instrucions from a lady to fit his car with a two-way radio; she had paid by cash and had covered the cost of the service for two years. This has saved Len miles of travelling for it means that, wherever he is, he can be reached and sent on the next rescue. It saves time and money, as well as wear and tear on him and the car. 'We'll never know who these wonderful people are. They bring tears to our eyes, their kindness is so great. We respect their desire to remain anonymous but if by chance you are reading this book, then from the bottom of our hearts Sheila and I say a very big thank you.'

That donations and letters now arrive from all over the world is in itself an indication of how Swan Rescue's reputation is spreading. Money comes from Africa, Asia and North America. One American couple on holiday in England posted their donation from Heathrow Airport; it was the last thing they did, they said, before returning to their Beverly Hills home. Their £100 donation has been followed by others from that part of the United States, so Len assumes that they must have spread the word.

Many letters come from Australia, where the Bakers lived happily for seven years and where they still have contacts and friends. One of their fondest memories of Australia is the black swan, rare in Britain, but prolific there and in New Zealand. 'They are beautiful birds, a little bit slimmer than our mute swans and a bit more aggressive. They live in large colonies, and one of my memories of Australia is the incredible noise that comes from these colonies. A terrific din. They aren't the placid, silent birds that we expect swans to be in this country.'

Any black swans in Britain will have been brought here from abroad: apparently there is a trade in importing black swans' eggs, for the cygnets are wanted as ornamental attraction on lakes and people will pay a fair sum for such an egg or cygnet.

Len couldn't believe his eyes when he saw a wild black swan on some waters near his home. Cobber, as he has been nicknamed, has joined a local flock, but how he got there nobody really knows. It is rumoured that a Norfolk man bought him and let him go free. 'I hope that story is true. It's a beautiful thing to have done. I've met Cobber, we stopped and had a chat. He's a typical Australian, very bold, and he likes a lot of open space around him. He decided when our talk was over – he just turned and went downstream. He'd finished with me.' So far Cobber hasn't been a patient of Len's, and in the nicest possible way Len will not mind if he never sees Cobber again.

It was the middle of the night and the telephone rang again, only this time the swans were too far away for Len and Sheila to be able to race to them. The caller was in Pakistan. He was worried about his swans; would Len go immediately to tend to them? They had heard that Len mended swans and he was needed urgently. It was out of the question, of course. Even if the caller had paid Len's expenses he could not have left his own swans for what would have been a trip of at least a week, probably longer. He offered to send them treatments. This wouldn't do. The caller was insistent: Len's presence was needed. The two of them argued back and forth until it was agreed that every day Len would channel his thoughts to Pakistan and pray for the swans' recovery. The caller felt that it was Len's intervention in the situation, not drugs, that was needed, and his spiritual presence would be better than nothing.

So every day, as promised, Len and Sheila both prayed for the sick swans, asking that they be allowed to live. Some time later the Pakistani telephoned again: 'The swans are very much better, thank you very much.' Mr Baker is obviously very influential!

121

Len's reputation with swans often leads people to think that he is in charge of, and somehow answerable for, their activities. This has its amusing side. Len remembers the time he was called to a council house in Norwich. A swan had crashlanded on a greenhouse roof and the owner had telephoned requesting Len's help. The swan was badly cut and stunned. He was young, not very experienced at flying, and had obviously been deceived by the moonlight on the glass roof into thinking that it was water. He was in a terrible state, completely covered in glass splinters, with larger chunks of glass sticking out of him in all directions. He looked like a hedgehog. Len began the slow task of picking out the glass bit by bit, the council tenant looking on.

The job took some time, and not until most of the glass was removed could Len risk picking up the swan.

'Who backs you?' asked the man.

'The general public,' replied Len.

'You're not a registered company then?'

'No.'

'In that case who are you insured with?'

'I'm not insured, why?' wondered Len.

A very angry man now demanded to know who the hell was going to pay for his broken greenhouse. If Len looked after swans then Len should pay, he insisted.

'Sue me,' were Len's parting words, as he picked up the swan and left.

It is not often that Len refuses to help a bird of any kind, but it was with some anger that he turned down a request to treat some geese in Scotland. The geese, apparently, had lead-poisoning, and having heard of Len's success in curing swans the callers wanted him to assist their geese. But Len discovered that their motives were not benevolent: they wanted the geese healthy and flying so they could shoot them. Not a game Len would play, and he told the men so in no uncertain terms.

Len Baker considers himself to be a man of the birds, especially swans, not a man of the people. His home, he says, is 'pure swan': from the front garden where the cygnets have their pens, through the house filled with scores of ornaments, paintings, sculptures and tapestries depicting swans; past the samples, the treatments, the elaborate records and files and Len's collection of swan books; through the kitchen where the very young cygnets sleep cosily at night, and into the back garden with the main swan pens and the caravan that acts as an operating theatre. If the telephone rings it is to do with swans. If he is invited to a meeting, or to address a group, the talk will be swans. He lives and breathes swans and has little time for anything else, certainly no time for what he regards as the selfish whims of humanity – the women who don't like bird droppings on their shoes and the men who want to shoot birds.

Len is gaining a reputation, but it is slow. He realises that he is not always his own best friend. As a man who thinks, and says, that committees are a waste of time, that scientists have no heart and don't care, he is not surprised that 'the establishment' – be they animal authorities, researchers or government bodies – have shunned him. But slowly these people are finding themselves unable to deny that the contribution Len is making to research into swans, especially with regard to lead-poisoning, is very valuable. Gradually he is being taken seriously: he is now invited to submit his findings to researchers, and he gets asked to sit on committees. Not that his attitude is changing. Rubbing shoulders with groups of people that once he stayed away from is something he will grin and bear for the sake of the swans. If doing so can broadcast the plight of the swans, then he will do it.

And underneath he is pleased that his work and dedication is slowly gaining recognition. He was untrained and unqualified when he began this work. All he had was love, plus physical and mental stamina. He learned as he went, discovering things the hard way, but he has carved a unique place for himself in the world of animal welfare. No one can ignore him now.

Having a reputation and a name to live up to does however become a responsibility in itself, and Len has had some embarrassing moments. There is a farmer in Suffolk who thinks that he is an absolute buffoon. Len had been called to a village by a woman who said there was a swan in distress near her general store. Len drove 75 miles and met the lady who, in her Land Rover, took him to a remote field. There in the middle of the field was a white duck. There was no swan. The woman apologised: 'I haven't lived in the country for long, I'm from London,' she explained. Having driven so many miles Len decided that he might as well take a look

123

at the duck, for it seemed rather strange that the bird should be sitting all alone in the middle of a field. He picked it up, tucked it under his arm, and made to leave the field to take the duck to some water. Suddenly he heard a booming voice:

'What are you doing with my so-and-so duck?'

It was a farmer with a loaded shotgun. 'That's my duck, are you stealing it?'

'No, no', stammered Len. The shotgun was aimed at him now. 'I'm not stealing it. I'm from Swan Rescue.'

'But that's a bloody duck.'

There was no reply to that. Len handed over the duck and fled.

The Future

This evening
As the day became tired,
A lone swan
Flew westward.
He took with him
Some dreams of mine.

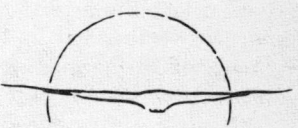

The swan, says Len, is the big white bird of warning. Because swans are so beautiful, and because in so many areas they are now conspicuous for their absence, they are drawing attention to the plight of birds in general. Ducks, geese and other water birds all suffer much the same fate as the swans. They are just as susceptible to the perils of lead; they bleed from hooks and line; they are victims of man's cruelty.

The big, majestic swan, with his huge wing-span and his grace and beauty, is issuing a warning. He is telling us, Len says, that the killing, the cruelty, the lack of care has got to come to an end. Humans must stop being selfish, must learn to share this planet, for every animal and bird has rights too. Swans are speaking up for the starlings in Piccadilly Circus, he says.

Some people may call Len Baker an alarmist. He maintains that swans will be extinct from our rivers within fifteen years unless something is done quickly to remedy the present situation. Other people, experts in their own areas of veterinary or animal welfare work, have told me that privately they agree with Mr Baker but their positions do not allow them to speak out.

What can be done? The major war has to be against the fishermen, for it is they who cause the most damage and death to swans in Britain. There are many things that Len would like to see done. First, an immediate ban on fishing in certain critical areas. The Nature Conservancy Council report also suggests this course of action, stating that areas where lead-poisoning is known to be particularly acute, such as Stratford-Upon-Avon, Reading and Nottingham, arrangements should be made between anglers and local authorities to designate 'no fishing' areas.

Preventing even more lead from being put into our rivers is obviously of vital importance too. The only way this can be achieved is for anglers to stop using lead weights, though sadly, for the moment at least, this is unlikely to happen. The NCC report called for a phasing out of lead within five years. The report was published in 1981 and to date Len says there is no evidence of this happening – indeed the number of lead deaths he comes across increase each year.

The advantages of lead to the fisherman are three fold: the metal is heavy, it is cheap, and it is malleable enough to be crimped easily on to the line. Research has been done into alternative substances but none so far meets these three requirements. Gold, silver and platinum would serve two of the needs but would be ridiculously expensive. Other materials produce other problems. A tungsten-based heavy putty substance has been considered, but apart from the fact that it could not be easily attached to the line, especially in cold and wet weather, it would also have to be marketed at something like five times the cost of lead. Stainless steel is another possibility; these weights are on sale at present in Britain but they do not find much favour with anglers, not least beause they cost nearly three times as much as lead.

An idea of coating lead weights with plastic had to be abandoned because the swan's gizzard is strong enough to erode the plastic, releasing the lead toxicity into its system.

Until a cheap, effective weight is produced it is unlikely that anglers will voluntarily move away from lead. About this Len Baker feels strongly. He does not think the swans should have to wait for voluntary action from anglers. He would like to see lead weights made illegal; he would like to see fishing clubs instruct their members not to use lead, with offenders being dismissed from the club; and he would like to see water authorities refuse rod licences to anyone found using lead. As for anglers who fish without a licence, Len maintains that those found guilty should face much heavier penalties than currently exist. The law must come down on the side of swans, he says; it should work to keep lead from our rivers.

The problem of hooks and line injuring swans could be solved almost immediately if anglers would only be more caring and considerate. If they took all their discarded tackle home with them rather than throwing it away on riverbanks, the suffering would diminish straight away.

The National Anglers' Council assures me that clubs are tightening up on their members' behaviour. Some are imposing suspensions on members who litter riverbanks. In fishing matches, when the fish are weighed, members may find their entry disqualified if there is evidence that they have littered the bank with tackle. NAC has also produced a code of conduct which is sent out by water authorities when they issue licences.

Unfortunately only one-third of anglers belong to a club. The rest fish alone without supervision, many without any direction or training. Some of these are children, some are holidays-only fishermen who don't know the rules or understand the dangers.

Better education, especially in the classroom, is something Len Baker would like to see – on conservation in general, but particularly on the relationship of waterfowl and angling, since so many children fish alone and are likely to go on fishing throughout their lives. The NAC has made a small beginning in the right direction, for in 1981 it launched a proficiency award scheme on coarse fishing to be run in schools among eleven to eighteen-years-olds. The scheme also touches on conservation. This is a start, although Len would like to see conservation as a compulsory subject on school curricula. Conservation, he holds, is not a subject any of us can opt out of. Schoolchildren should have to study it, just as they do English or maths. Conservation must be taken seriously in schools, for the future of our wildlife relies on future generations and their behaviour.

There is a fine line between cruelty and carelessness, and Len maintains that if the law was tougher in protecting the animals, humans would be more careful. If an angler casts at a swan and blinds it, is that cruelty or carelessness? Sometimes, if there are witnesses, it may be obvious, but all too often it is difficult to know the truth. But if people knew that the penalty would be severe should they accidentally injure a swan they would automatically take more care. And the person who deliberately injures swans would, one hopes, be less likely to risk such cruelty if the penalty was something to fear. Len often tells with glee the tale of a man in Russia who was sent to prison for 2½ years for injuring a swan. While he does not expect such penalities ever to exist in Britain he would nevertheless like to see the law tightened up. People are of course prosecuted from time to time, but as the law stands at the moment it is difficult to prove cruelty against a wild bird.

Two years ago a young ornithologist saw two men by the side of a reservoir shooting at whooper swans. The young lad asked nearby golfers to keep an eye on the men while he ran off to fetch the police. The two men were arrested, and subsequently pleaded guilty at Bolton Magistrates Court and one of them was fined £550 plus £20 costs for killing one swan and injuring another; the second man was fined £50 plus £20 costs for trespassing with a firearm. Although the police do on occasion take out prosecutions for offences against birds, it was probably because the men were armed and firing in an area used by the public that the police responded so quickly. The other important aspect of this case was that the swans were visiting whoopers and they enjoy slightly more protection under the law than do our own mute swans.

The Wildlife and Countryside Act, 1981 (of which the laws concerning wild birds came into force in September 1982) does give the mute swan full protection under the law but with some let-out clauses for landowners. A person is not guilty of an offence if he can prove that the killing of the swan, or swans, was necessary because serious damage was being done to his livestock or crops. The key words here are 'necessary' and 'serious'. Swans, it is true, are capable of devastating a field of seedling wheat, and they paddle in mud and can ruin the chances of young seed, but there would have to be a great many swans before the damage could be called serious. And a landowner should use scaring tactics before resorting to the shotgun.

Len Baker maintains that farmers do not always try alternatives before the gun. He has heard many rumours of farmers shooting swans, indeed one rumoured massacre numbered as high as 40

128

birds. But gathering proof against such a farmer is difficult, for at least one witness is necessary and that person has got to be prepared to give evidence in court. Anyone guilty of an illegal shooting usually buries the bodies, thereby destroying evidence. News of such killings filters slowly through the village community and by the time it reaches a body that might prosecute – the Royal Society for the Protection of Birds, for example – the witnesses have scattered or have got their stories muddled.

A new licensing provision has been introduced with the 1981 Act. A farmer may now apply to the Ministry of Agriculture, Fisheries and Food (MAFF) for a special licence giving him permission to kill in order to 'prevent' damage to his crops. This is a potentially controversial area, and it is to be hoped that the Ministry will refuse such licences until the farmer can prove he has tried all other means, including scaring tactics.

The maximum fine for cruelty to mute swans is £200 for each offence, the fine multiplying with each swan or egg involved. This applies to anything from destroying nests and stealing eggs to cruelty or killing. 'It's bloody ridiculous,' says Len. 'There should be imprisonment, say three months, for the hurting or killing of a swan or any wild bird. Or perhaps some kind of compulsory conservation work like three months of clearing lead from banks or some back-breaking river clearance.' A special plea from Len is that should you ever accidentally hurt a swan or damage a nest, do not slink off home. Inform your local RSPCA office, or telephone Len himself on 0603 29444, you need not even give him your name, just say what has happened and where.

If it is necessary that the power cables carrying our electricity should for technical reasons remain above ground, surely some kind of warning device for birds could be erected on a nationwide basis. Len suggests luminous discs, spaced at regular intervals. The Central Electricity Generating Board tell me that they and the regional electricity authorities will attach aluminium bulges along the cables but only if specifically asked to do so by the public. If you care, please ask – in fact demand – that your local electricity board do this. Bulges are better than nothing, but luminous alerting systems, either discs or coils, are better still.

Birds fly at night-time, too, when bulges are of little help so something luminous is needed.

The accessibility of certain lethal weapons is also a problem. The law is strict in some areas but lax in others. A licence from the police has to be obtained for the purchase and possession of shotguns, rifles, pistols, revolvers and certain especially dangerous air weapons. The police are very diligent as to who is granted a licence, and owners of licences guard them jealously. They know that if they were to behave irresponsibly, for example in allowing a youngster to use their weapon, they would probably lose their licence – a risk that most holders would not take.

It is the air weapons that cause Len, and the swans, most distress, for here restrictions are limited and the purchase of these potentially lethal weapons is easy. If you are seventeen or over you may buy or hire most types of airguns and airrifles, and their ammunition, without a licence. Once you own an air weapon you may give it, or lend it, to anyone over the age of fourteen. The flow of these weapons into the hands of youngsters is therefore unrestricted and perfectly legal. (They also get into the hands of the under-fourteens, although that is illegal.)

Airguns can kill swans and other birds and animals, whether that was the users' intention or not. Len has had cases where swans have obviously been used as target practice. If the swans are not killed outright they often linger on for days in pain, often dying with the pellets still embedded in their bodies.

Airrifles can be bought easily in shops up and down the country; they can even be obtained through mail-order catalogues. One catalogue was recently selling a high-powered .22 airrifle for £99.95, or £2.63 a week for 38 weeks. It is therefore not beyond youngsters to buy such a gun out of their pocket-money, for although catalogues carry a warning that it is illegal to make such a purchase if you are under seventeen, there is nothing to stop someone else buying on the youngster's behalf.

But it is not, of course, only the under-seventeens who accidentally, or deliberately, aim at swans. Such behaviour comes in all age-groups, including adults. Len wants the availability of these weapons restricted and the use of them only allowed with a licence. 'Every Christmas these lethal weapons are in kids' stockings, it's crazy. They are killers, they shouldn't be in

130

children's hands, nothing that kills should be in a child's hands. Let kids be kids, whatever happened to scrumping and knock-down-ginger? We shouldn't be giving them weapons that kill birds and maim humans.'

The same sentiment applies to crossbows, for there are no restrictions on these nor are they expensive to buy. A crossbow suitable for a young teenager costs in the region of £60-£70. The bolts inflict much pain and suffering, often leading to a slow death. The swan that Len found crucified to a tree had been shot with a crossbow. And Pawline, Marlon's mate, was killed by a crossbow bolt.

But what can be done about deliberate human cruelty? It seems as if no laws or licences will bring that to an end. Nothing would have stopped the person who threw thirteen pub darts into the back of a swan. Len saw the swan in the reeds, where it had gone out of human reach to die. What had it ever done, what offence had it ever given to anyone, what wrong had it committed to earn it such a painful, degrading death?

Len maintains that even the people who are meant to be working for animals are largely ineffective. Some individuals within organizations such as the RSPCA and the RSPB, to name just two, care and do as much as they can, but even they have their hands tied by the bureaucratic systems that prevail within such large societies, trusts and funds. He claims that these organizations lack muscle and drive, that they waste public donations and waste time on projects that are meaningless and could be done much quicker. An effective body of welfare organizations should have more influence on changing the law, he maintains.

Len Baker would like to see all animal and bird welfare groups abolished and replaced by a kind of animals' national health service. He is the first to admit he himself is not an administrator, nor a planner, nor an economist, nor even a vet, but he is sure that if the knowledgeable, caring people put their heads together such a scheme could be devised. It could be run, nation-wide, on the public funds that already pour in to the various charities. It would be staffed by veterinary experts who would have the necessary back-up of nursing and field staff. It would have clinics and hospitals, and provide sanctuaries for wild animals. Pet-owners would be able to use the service too, having to bear only a small prescription charge for drugs.

The trouble with societies at the moment, at least as far as wild birds are concerned, is that they appear to be non-existent. Prosecutions are few and far between. Half the staff never leave the offices and actually go out into the fields and touch a bird. There's too much emphasis on glossy brochures and gift systems. I think there's a danger when you put animal welfare people into uniforms and give them ranks. If you work with animals or birds then your job isn't to sit at a desk writing papers, it's to be handling the animal or bird, caring for it, getting it better. I'd like to know how many people in these large organizations have actually sat up all night with a dying bird. I bet hardly any of them have – for a start they clock off at 5.30.

The whole emphasis of animal welfare in this country has got to change. The general public gives thousands of pounds, but how much of it I wonder actually gets spent on the animals or birds? Birds don't want carpeted reception areas and beautiful secretaries answering telephones that co-ordinate with the wallpaper. They want splints put on their broken wings, they want lead removed from their bodies and hooks taken out of their windpipes. Swans are choking and bleeding to death, they are feeling sick and giddy on our rivers; how does a computerized communication system help them?

They desperately need a proper system of hospitals and sanctuaries where they can be treated instantly when they need it and can then convalesce and live safely out of harm's way. It's Utopia maybe, but as far as the birds and animals are concerned it's a vital necessity.

Karlee, Marlon's granddaughter, was destined to have a short stay on this earth, but during this time she played on Len's and Sheila's emotions. A bad case of lead-poisoning, she had arrived at the Bakers' home unable to walk or eat. Every day Sheila had spent a couple of hours with her, and on one gloriously happy day Karlee started to walk again. But the delight was short-lived. At 7.30 one morning little Karlee, just three months old, died in Sheila's lap as she sat on the kitchen floor. It broke Sheila's heart.

All the swans matter, but this was Marlon's granddaughter, and fate was slowly taking from them all links with their beloved Marlon.

A post-mortem showed that Karlee had 602 parts per million of lead in her kidney. It took five weeks to kill her. 'She didn't stand a chance. She inherited lead from her mum; she was dying as soon as she was born.'

So the heartache goes on. At this very moment, as you are reading, Len is probably on a riverbank somewhere tending to a swan, or Sheila is at home giving comfort to a dying friend. They hope and pray that Karlee's brother and sister, the great Khan and Krista, are not on their list of forthcoming patients. They've already treated them once. Khan, when she was four months old, got a fish-hook in each leg; and Krista at eight weeks old had a piece of fishing line, with a hook and lead attached, caught in her throat. Khan only had to stay with the Bakers for four days, and Len was able to treat Krista on the riverbank. Khan and Krista, the last of six cygnets belonging to Karla and Karl II, were sent on their merry way by their parents in the winter of 1982. Karl II and Karla are still living near Marlon's and Pawline's nesting site by the 7 knots speed limit sign, and let us hope that in the gap between the completion of this book and your reading it nothing will have happened to them.

But during the writing of this book Len has fulfilled two personal dreams, both of which he was for ever being told were impossible.

During all the years of treating lead-poisoned swans it had become blatantly obvious that the best cure of all was to get the lead out of the swan's gizzard. As already explained, surgery is not feasible, for although it is possible few vets would relish cutting into the muscular framework of the gizzard. A pump, similar to a stomach pump used on humans, was what was needed. Investigations revealed that the only device currently available that could be adapted for the purpose cost several thousands of pounds, so that was immediately ruled out.

Len sought help from brother Bob, who apart from being by trade a heating and ventilation engineer and by inclination an artist is also good at all things mechanical. The problem Len set him was this: I need a machine that will remove lead weights from

133

a swan's gizzard but will not involve me in having to put the swan under anaesthetic and won't cause the swan too much anxiety. It must also be cheap to make.

Within weeks Bob arrived with the gizzard pump. He had begged and borrowed bits and pieces, including a pump, and the whole thing had totalled £250.

> I knew that whatever you make you can't expect it to work first time, so we spent a whole night practising in the kitchen. As a substitute gizzard we used a bottle in which we placed some sand, grit and pieces of lead. To our dismay the pump sucked out everything except the lead. We were shattered, but soon realised that of course the glass sides of the bottle weren't giving under the pressure created by the pumping, so everything was coming out except the lead, which was too heavy. But we were confident that a gizzard would give under the pressure.

So it was decided to try the pump on a swan, and by chance I was with Len and Bob on the day that was to be an important landmark in the caring of swans in this country. A lead-poisoned swan was chosen and gently held in position. Two tubes were inserted down its throat and into the gizzard, one tube sucking out the contents of the gizzard while the other tube flushed in water. 'It didn't cause too much distress; we were surprised how easy it was.' The contents of the swan's gizzard were brought into the kitchen and I watched as they were carefully filtered through one of Sheila's old nylon stockings.

The fine sand passed through quickly, leaving the larger pieces of grit. With tweezers Len prodded the grit, with Sheila, Bob and myself looking on. Suddenly – eureka! There they were, four pieces of anglers' lead shot. The experiment had been very successful. And suddenly I was the outsider as husband and wife and brother hugged each other, tears of joy filling their eyes.

In theory no swan need ever die from lead-poisoning again. The reality is somewhat different, for the lead has got to be removed very shortly after it has been swallowed. The whole process relies on quick diagnosis followed up by swift action. As far as we know Len's pumping machine is the only one in the country, and he is the only person who has come anywhere near so close to solving lead-poisoning. The pump has since been used many times, with great success. Sometimes a swan has been too ill to be saved, for once lead is in the blood, kidney, liver and bones, death is very near – although even then it may not be too late, for modern drugs that fight the lead are more effective if the lead itself has been removed from the gizzard. The lives of many swans have been saved by this machine already, and many lead-free birds have been returned to their water and skies.

But Len still felt that there was another side to the problem. Given that under current circumstances it is impossible to stop swans from getting lead-poisoning, a better solution than curing them would be to give them a safe, lead-free place of their own, away from boats and anglers, in which to live. Len had dreamed of this for a long while when one morning, as he was browsing through his local paper, he saw an advertisement: 14.2 acres of river frontage with pasture and woodland, for sale by auction. His heart skipped a beat. He telephoned the agent and was told that the land was expected to sell for around £30,000. A despondent Len did not bother to put an offer in writing; there was no point, for he had no money. But he could not get that land out of his mind.

He knew where it was, only a ten-minute car ride from his home. He knew the river that bordered the land was safe; it was away from the holidaymakers' usual areas and there was no fishing. He had to get the land. He managed to discover who the owners were and telephoned them direct.

'What do you want the land for?' he was asked. Len explained.

'Then for God's sake get to your bank manager,' the owner said, adding that he would let Len have it for £22,000.

'I talked to the swans and they agreed. They'd got to have some safe water and everything was pointing to this particular piece. They'd *got* to have it.'

Len telephoned his bank manager that afternoon and said he needed £22,000. An appointment was made for him to go in and discuss the matter a week later. A trembling Len and Sheila went to try to persuade the bank that their investment was for a good cause. Len had no money of his own; he could not even contribute a few hundred, let alone a few thousand. Eight minutes later the

135

bank, the Midland at Norwich where Len has both his personal account and the swans' account, had agreed to give him a personal loan. The monthly repayments amount to £560. 'I never know from one month to the next where I'll get that money from, but I always do. The swans fix it. We've been living like this for six years and something always happens to save us. If it's right for the swans then fate steps in, it's as simple as that.'

The land has been called Marlon Land, and it is a permanent monument to the memory of that wonderful swan which befriended them during the early dark days of the Swan Rescue Service. Len has taken a cutting from the willow that kisses the water where Marlon and Pawline first mated, and there is now a new willow growing in Marlon Land.

It is a little piece of England that belongs to the swans. It's their sanctuary, no one can take it from them, no one can hurt them there. They have got a quarter-mile of river that has no lead in it, no boats, and I will never allow fishing. I am buying it for them. No one can ever accuse them of trespassing, for it's theirs.

Slowly Marlon Land is being fenced off so that straying members of the public can not happen upon it. Already five ponds have been dug and some 160 swans are making their home there. The healthy ones come and go as they wish, but Len has made it the permanent home for his crippled swans. Rather than keep them in his garden he is now able to let them see out their days in this sanctuary. Currently some 60 invalided swans are settling in.

We're having to wean them off grain and back on to natural vegetation; we're doing it slowly, but they learn very quickly. So many of them had got used to us bringing them their food that now they have got to learn to be swans again and go out and find their dinner. Some of them go crazy with excitement, they can't believe that they are seeing food everywhere they look.

One such swan was Blakeney. She had been hit in the throat by

136

an oar which had broken her neck, and to this day a vertebra still sticks out of the back of her neck.

All she did at first was eat, eat, eat. She went bananas. She is ruining her figure – she's very over-weight – but she is happy and that's, all that counts. And she is in love; nothing has happened yet but she has definitely got her eye on one of the swans that flew into the sanctuary of his own free will.

It's so funny watching the swans sizing each other up. The males parade up and down looking at the talent, and turning to each other as if to say 'I don't think much of yours'. And the females turn their backs on them and carry on talking amongst themselves.

It is pure magic to watch them. There is definitely a selection process going on; they have attractions for certain swans and not others, that's quite obvious. And when they've decided who their partner will be it is pure and wonderful – nothing crude, it's beautiful.

Once Len realizes that a pair want to team up he gives them privacy in a pen of their own, and some protection from foxes who could be tempted to eat the cygnets. But one of the aims of the sanctuary is to help the birds become wild again. Len does not intend to feed them; he thinks it is wrong that swans have become reliant upon white bread from humans. He has given them safety and territory, and believes that the rest is up to them.

Anyone who is really ecology minded wants to see animals left alone in peace in their natural environments. Sometimes being a goody-goody can be wrong. If you find an injured bird or baby animal it is sometimes best to leave it. The chances are its mum knows where it is and what's happened and she is best equipped to help it. Taking it home and keeping it in a cardboard box can be unkind. It has become fashionable to be a conservationist, but the best help humans can give wildlife is to leave it alone. If you see a hedgehog in the road that is in danger of being squashed by a car then of course, carry it to the side and place it out of danger; but don't go around the countryside collecting hedgehogs and putting them in your garden because that way *you* feel happier for them. It is only because man has interfered with swans and their natural habitats that they are in the terrible state that they are in now. If you want to be a caring person then mind your own business, let wildlife get on with its life and don't interfere.

Speeding down the M11 on his way to London, the last thing a lorry driver expects to land in front of him is a swan. But that is exactly what happened to one man some months ago. The swan, presumably thinking that the road was a river, landed amongst the traffic. The kind-hearted lorry driver, from Norwich, swung his lorry around to block the path of oncoming traffic and retrieved the injured swan. He knew about Len and the Swan Rescue Service, but his commitments did not allow him to turn round immediately and head back to Norwich, so he sat the swan by the heater to keep it warm and took it to London.

On the way home he bought it a pork pie in a transport café, and on returning to Norwich in the evening he took the swan straight to Len. 'He's had a nice day out in London,' he assured Len. 'He's seen the sights!'

This very lucky swan had escaped its ordeal with just a dislocated leg and is one of the swans now convalescing in Marlon Land. Amongst its new friends are a swan from Essex which nearly choked to death when a four-inch fishing float got caught in its throat; a blind swan which is suffering from botulism, and his ladyfriend who has a .22 air-rifle pellet embedded in the front of her head. Both the last two swans will die soon; they were in such pain, and with such odds against them improving, that Len had intended having them put to sleep.

Never for one moment has Len ceased to believe that he was guided to this work. Whether it was God, fate, the swans themselves, or all three he does not know, but he has always felt that something has been showing him the way forward at every step. Nor has he ever ceased to believe in the simple philosophy that in order to understand swans he had to live with them.

There is a North American Indian legend which, paraphrased, goes something like this: 'When the earth is sick and the animals disappear, the warriors of the rainbow will come to protect the wildlife and heal the earth.' The warriors, ordinary people from ordinary backgrounds, will form a rainbow because they will be of many races and religions. Len Baker is one such warrior, and indeed he has been a fighter, as his record shows.

Like so many of us, he once trusted that the various national and international animal organizations were doing the job of protecting our wildlife that we thought we were paying them to do. But they seem to have been negligent in this responsibility. The world's endangered and threatened species lists continue to grow: several thousand animals are considered to be endangered or threatened, and some 200 mammals, including the blue whale, the tiger, the rhino and the elephant, are thought to be under imminent threat of extinction. The ordinary people of the world are now crying 'Enough is enough, the slaughter must stop.' The more they learn the more they are horrified by what has been done, and is still being done, in the name of mankind.

Len Baker is a warrior of the rainbow. He is one of the growing movement of individuals who are not prepared to leave it to the experts any more. He is trying to do something about it himself.

We are very wary of the majority of so-called professionals who are probably well schooled in the technicalities and mechanics of the wild bird but we have found only a few who really care about the swan as a living, feeling being.

We belong to that band of people described by professionals as cranks. We are proud of the title. For if to be a crank is to prefer the company of birds to the company of humans then we openly admit we are cranks.

Let's face it, to spend all your money on a bird is not normal, or sensible. To speed around Norfolk with a car full of swans is not the action of a sane person. We should be spending our money on beer, or a two-week holiday in Majorca, or an electric carving knife.

We believe that we are, without doubt, the luckiest and

richest people on earth. We are all guilty of taking from this planet, we in our way are trying to put something back. The swan has repaid us a thousandfold; we are indebted to him, not him to us. He has taught us more about honesty and loyalty than any human, and as a bonus he has allowed us into his world.

We shall continue to be cranks.

What future lies before Len Baker and the swans is not certain. The cost of running Swan Rescue continues to rise, and while the fight to raise money goes on the needs of the swans do not diminish. The 'experts' maintain that it does not matter if the swans vanish from many of our rivers because they are breeding happily in other places. But this is not a philosophy that interests Len. He knows a place where you can see hundreds of swans, but you will need a Land Rover to get to it. The grace and beauty of the swans was given to us all to enjoy, but man has abused the trust and soon he may not be be able to gaze upon these legendary creatures any more.

Len asked me if it would be possible to leave the last few pages of this book blank, as a symbolic gesture to the swans' future. I decided, however, that it would be more fitting to end the book with something Len once wrote himself. He, after all, is the expert: he has witnessed the horror of it all.

There must be a place where the swans can live in peace and away from the hurt that some humans inflict.

We could learn so much from them but it seems we are too busy trying to keep pace with so-called progress. Sheila and I try to stand back from the world; our needs are frugal, we have grown to prefer the company of swans.

The swan is a thief, but a very clever thief. He stole our love, our time, our every waking hour. He stole our money, our holidays, our future and our dreams, and he was so clever he left us happier for the crime. He is the perfect parent, the perfect flyer, the perfect warrior but the epitome of peace. And we, the all-knowing human, call him an animal!

When the darkness touches our lives and the song of life no

longer sings in us we hope we can leave the earth with the dignity of a swan.

On a sun-kissed day on a stretch of river a swan will be seen sitting quietly with his own reflection; the whiteness of his plumage dazzles and the orange of his bill is a beautiful contrast to the lime green of the reeds. Here is perfection. We must keep this, at the cost of our very lives. We will keep it, we owe it to them.

When the cygnets fly for the first time and feel freedom and you are lucky enough to witness their magic, take the experience and savour it, for it is their gift to you. It is all they have to give. When the swans' wings and the wind give out their music it is a haunting sound, it is the very sound of freedom. May you be blessed with this experience, you will certainly be richer for it.

We are.

St Francis of Assisi said that not to hurt our humble brethren is our first duty to them, but to stop there is not enough. We have a higher mission – to be of service to them whenever they require it. Len Baker is doing his best.

Len Baker's Acknowledgments

How can I begin to thank the people who have helped Sheila and me nearly every step of the way: the technical experts, such as Dr Ian Keymer at the MAFF veterinary investigation centre at Norwich, Mike French at the Institute of Terrestrial Ecology, and my local vet, Mr Barnes, all of whom have shown patience and understanding as they guided me through their individual areas of expertise; and the friends who stuck by us in the dark days as well as the good, so many that I hesitate to name a few for fear of leaving some dear people out. Thank you all, for everything.

My thanks, too, to those North American Indians, Oskanonton (known as Jimmy Green) and Pammahetchka (known as Running Lady) who saw it all long before I did.

My loving thanks to Sheila, for I could not have done it without her.

And finally my thanks to the current Swan Rescue team, upon whom I, and the swans, have come to rely: Ron and Rose Collins, Paul and Sue Scheller, Eddie Bush, Rina Milsom, Peter Nicholls, Jason 'Corkie' Cork, Bob Woodbridge, Bob and Lyn Baker, Bert and Joyce Green.

If, having read this book, you would like to help save the swans, your donations will be gratefully received. My address is: Swan Rescue Service, Shotesham St Mary, Nr. Norwich, Norfolk. Thank you.

Len Baker

DOWN THE VILLAGE STREET
by Peter Douglas

An uproarious chronicle of a year's doings and happenings in a small Norfolk country village that is a riot from beginning to end. A worthy companion to the stories of James Herriot and Neil Boyd.

'It hit Maggie and I that we had really done it. For better or worse we were now heading for the rural life, the quiet village, the daydream existence. I stopped the car, and looked at Maggie. "We've really done it," I said. She smiled. "I know," she said. "You can keep all your factories and chimneys, and your motor-ways and smog. This is what I want to see every day." We both looked at the quiet countryside around us. "Yes," I agreed. "To hell with the city." "Yes," said Maggie. "And to hell with the three-legged cat." . . .'

'It is blessed with a similar whimsical appeal (as the Herriot and Boyd books) and a strong whiff of future success . . . brims over with joy.'
Sunday Express

0 552 11256 9   95p

A SELECTED LIST OF NON-FICTION TITLES AVAILABLE FROM CORGI BOOKS

WHILE EVERY EFFORT IS MADE TO KEEP PRICES LOW, IT IS SOMETIMES NECESSARY TO INCREASE PRICES AT SHORT NOTICE. CORGI BOOKS RESERVE THE RIGHT TO SHOW AND CHARGE NEW RETAIL PRICES ON COVERS WHICH MAY DIFFER FROM THOSE ADVERTISED IN THE TEXT OR ELSEWHERE.

THE PRICES SHOWN BELOW WERE CORRECT AT THE TIME OF GOING TO PRESS.

☐	99091 4	Animals in War	Jilly Cooper	£2.95
☐	99012 4	Intelligent and Loyal	Jilly Cooper	£2.50
☐	11256 9	Down the Village Street	Peter Douglas	95p
☐	12033 2	Diary of a Medical Nobody	Kenneth Lane	£1.75
☐	12465 6	West Country Doctor	Kenneth Lane	£1.95
☐	12399 4	Any Fool Can Be a Pig Farmer	James Robertson	£1.75
☐	12577 6	Place of Stones	Ruth Janette Ruck	£1.95
☐	98051 X	The Complete Book of Self-Sufficiency	John Seymour	£6.95
☐	99059 0	The Lore of the Land	John Seymour	£4.95
☐	12525 3	Two for Joy	Joyce Stranger	£1.75
☐	10927 4	Two's Company	Joyce Stranger	£1.50
☐	11803 6	How to Own a Sensible Dog	Joyce Stranger	£1.25
☐	98013 7	Ireland, A Terrible Beauty (illus)	Jill & Leon Uris	£6.95
☐	99090 6	Ireland Revisited (illus)	Jill Uris	£7.95
☐	10907 X	Hovel in the Hills	Elizabeth West	£1.50
☐	11707 2	Garden in the Hills	Elizabeth West	£1.25
☐	12072 3	Kitchen in the Hills	Elizabeth West	£1.50
☐	12513 X	Suffer Little Children	Elizabeth West	£1.75

All these books are available at your bookshop or newsagent, or can be ordered direct from the publisher. Just tick the titles you want and fill in the form below.

CORGI BOOKS, Cash Sales Department, P.O. Box 11, Falmouth, Cornwall.

Please send cheque or postal order, no currency.

Please allow cost of book(s) plus the following for postage and packing:

U.K. CUSTOMERS—Allow 55p for the first book, 22p for the second book and 14p each additional book ordered, to a maximum charge of £1.75.

B.F.P.O. and Eire—Allow 55p for the first book, 22p for the second book plus 14p per copy for the next seven books, thereafter 8p per book.

Overseas Customers—Allow £1.00 for the first book and 25p per copy for each additional book.

NAME (Block Letters) ....

ADDRESS ....

....